What People Are Saying About Glamour Girls:

"I devoured this book. It is the perfect guided tour for beauty without having an agenda to sell you anything except God's truths about the real you. Glamour tip: don't buy another magazine—trust me. I am forever changed."

—Tammy Trent, national recording artist; author

"*Glamour Girls* will help you grasp the fact that what you decide to eat will determine how your body, mind, and soul will function. Proper nutrition is the framework for your real beauty inside and out."

—Tricia Bland, RD, CPC; owner, L.E.A.N. Consulting

"Andrea's easy-to-understand yet diverse approach to physical fitness hits all the vital areas. She proves that fitness is absolutely necessary, doesn't have to cost a fortune, and can be totally fun!"

—Carla O'Brien, certified personal trainer

"My favorite part of *Glamour Girls* has been learning what colors look best on me, which hairstyles work with my face shape, how to stand gracefully when I sing in front of a group, and how to do my very own manicure! Thanks, Aunt Andrea!"

—Katie Spellman, teen B.A.B.E.

The B.A.B.E. Book Series:

"In Hollywood, it doesn't take long to identify the world's beauty standard: tall and thin with clear skin and perfect hair is best. Right? Wrong. Andrea's B.A.B.E. series get to the heart of the matter: beauty isn't beauty unless it starts on the inside. Wanna be gorgeous? Be a B.A.B.E.!"

—Cheryl Ladd, actress (original *Charlie's Angels*); author, *Token Chick*

"I'm the mother of three sons, and I wish every girl they knew would read Andrea's books to gain wisdom on becoming the kind of girl you would want your sons to meet! Andrea's insights will help young women avoid the pain and pitfalls of life and step into the promises of God!"

—Pam Farrel, author, *Men Are Like Waffles, Women Are Like Spaghetti* and *Got Teens?*

"Andrea Stephens is a stunning person inside and out, and this is reflected in her books. They're written in a fun style, and reading them feels like I'm sampling chocolate. They're cool tools to put in the hands of young women as they face the cultural definition of beauty and acceptance. TLhey tip girls to the truth of finding who they are and what image really means."

—**Suzanne Eller, author; speaker**

"Andrea's insights and writing style are right on target for teen girls and women."

—**H. Norm Wright, licensed Christian therapist; author of more than seventy books, including** *"Let's Just Be Friends"* **and** *Starting Out Together*

The B.A.B.E. Seminar™:

"I love The B.A.B.E. Seminar™! Andrea has designed a first-class, refreshing event that helps young women discover God's truth about themselves. From beauty and boys to purity and peer pressure, this seminar addresses key issues and concerns in a way that's uniquely *teen* and uniquely *girl*."

—**Lisa Velthouse, former Brio Girl; author,** *Saving My First Kiss*

"With practical advice on topics like how to apply makeup, and important insights into subjects like how to discover and use your spiritual gifts, Andrea encourages and motivates girls to be all that God wants them to be."

—**Shannon Kubiak Primicerio, author,** *The Divine Dance*, *God Called a Girl*, **and the Being a Girl series**

"The B.A.B.E. Seminar™ gave our girls a fresh perspective on what real beauty is all about and how God has uniquely designed each one of them to be his own special B.A.B.E.! To top it all off, several girls made first-time commitments to Christ. I would recommend Andrea Stephens and The B.A.B.E. Seminar™."

—**Danny Curry, youth minister, Greenfield, Indiana**

"Andrea knows know to connect with girls. While addressing the serious realities that teenage girls are facing, she does it in her own fun-loving and gentle style."

—**David, associate pastor, Pennsylvania**

"There was a tremendous response from our community that indicated a need and a hunger for relevant, biblical input into girls' lives. Every city—no matter the size—would benefit from offering The B.A.B.E. Seminar™."

—**Marcus, youth director, Michigan**

Campbell ~

Shine for Jesus!

You are a

BABE!

XO

Andrea

Stephen

GLAMOUR GIRLS

Other books by Andrea Stephens

GLAMOUR GIRLS

The B.A.B.E. Handbook to Real Beauty

ANDREA STEPHENS

Revell
Grand Rapids, Michigan

© 2006 by Andrea Stephens

Published by Fleming H. Revell
a division of Baker Publishing Group
P.O. Box 6287, Grand Rapids, MI 49516-6287
www.revellbooks.com

Printed in the United States of America

Library of Congress Cataloging-in-Publication Data
Stephens, Andrea.
    Glamour girls : the B.A.B.E. handbook to real beauty / Andrea Stephens.
        p.   cm. — (A B.A.B.E. book)
    ISBN 10: 0-8007-5968-0 (pbk.)
    ISBN 978-0-8007-5968-1 (pbk.)
    1. Teenage girls—Religious life. 2. Beauty, Personal. 3. Body, Human—Religious aspects—Christianity. 4. Self-perception. I. Title. II. Series: Stephens, Andrea. B.A.B.E. book.
BV4551.3.S737 2006
248.8′33—dc22
                                                2006010170

Scripture marked AMP is taken from the Amplified® Bible, Copyright © 1954, 1958, 1962, 1964, 1965, 1987 by The Lockman Foundation. Used by permission.

Scripture marked Message is taken from *The Message* by Eugene H. Peterson, copyright © 1993, 1994, 1995, 2000, 2001, 2002. Used by permission of NavPress Publishing Group. All rights reserved.

Scripture marked NASB is taken from the New American Standard Bible®, Copyright © 1960, 1962, 1963, 1968, 1971, 1972, 1973, 1975, 1977, 1995 by The Lockman Foundation. Used by permission.

Scripture marked NIV is taken from the HOLY BIBLE, NEW INTERNATIONAL VERSION®. NIV®. Copyright © 1973, 1978, 1984 by International Bible Society. Used by permission of Zondervan. All rights reserved.

Scripture marked NLT is taken from the *Holy Bible*, New Living Translation, copyright © 1996. Used by permission of Tyndale House Publishers, Inc., Wheaton, Illinois 60189. All rights reserved.

Scripture marked TLB is taken from *The Living Bible*, copyright © 1971. Used by permission of Tyndale House Publishers, Inc., Wheaton, Illinois 60189. All rights reserved.

Portions of this book are based on material from the author's previous works in La Glamour (*Brio* magazine) and in *Bloom: A Girl's Guide to Growing Up*.

The B.A.B.E. Seminar™: Beautiful, Accepted, Blessed, Eternally Significant® is a registered trademark of Andrea Stephens Ministries.

Published in association with the literary agency of Alive Communications, Inc., 7680 Goddard Street, Suite 200, Colorado Springs, CO 80920.

interior design by brian brunsting

To Alisa.
You share my love for
a day at the beach or a day at the spa;
a chance to wear sequins or a chance to wear sweats;
and a giant chocolate muffin or a good workout.
And you share my deepest desire—to know God's Word
and to be the B.A.B.E.s he has called us to be.
Thanks for being my sister and my friend.

Inside
GLAMOUR GIRLS

HOW CLASSY OF YOU!

I feel like Moses—you know, the burning-bush, parting-the-Red-Sea guy! He won his battle, but it was not possible without his brother and good friend helping him. He needed them to come alongside him so he could do what God asked him to do. It was one of those "wind beneath my wings" moments.

Same with me. Completing the B.A.B.E. Book series became a bit of a battle. There was the Guatemala mission trip, The B.A.B.E. Seminar™ in London, and the cross-country move from Bakersfield, California, to Ft. Myers, Florida (my husband was called to a new church). There was Wilma—as in *hurricane* (we had no electricity for a week, but I found out that Sterno makes a great indoor camp-fire), another B.A.B.E. Seminar™, company, two conferences, and, of course, Christmas!

I have known that this series was an assignment from the throne. I have completed the assignment. I pray he will say, "Well done." But the "attagirl" won't be just for me. On this final book, my friends came alongside and helped! Carol spent hours compiling info. Suzette found definitions and websites. Tricia made sure my nutrition and fitness info was accurate. Bill made several dinners—and rubbed my shoulders. And many prayed! The Lord used each of you to help sustain me during these hectic and trying few months. To each of you I offer sincere thanks. It was very cool of you to hold me up during this time.

Special thanks to Jennifer Leep at Revell and Beth Jusino at Alive Communications. You are both real B.A.B.E.s!

THE B.A.B.E. JOURNEY

Once upon a time, there was a small-town girl who grew up loving fashion, makeup, and glittery jewelry. As a teen she had starstruck eyes! She wanted to be either Miss America or on the cover of *Vogue*!

Okay, this isn't really a fairy tale. It's my life.

I wanted the lights, the lenses, and the limos! I went for the pageant thing first. I polished up my guitar performance, improved my grades, read up on current events, and entered the Junior Miss Scholarship Program. I finished second in the state pageant. A few years later, I entered the Miss Oklahoma Pageant. Second again! Therefore, not being a state winner with obligations, I switched gears and prepared for a modeling convention scheduled for later that summer. Well, the Miss America dream was put on hold because the trip to New York City won me a contract with Wilhelmina Models, Inc.

I was thrilled. I packed my bags and moved to the city a few weeks later.

I was ready. I settled into a small apartment with several other models, then took to the streets for my go-sees (that's model talk for the word *interview*—you'd go see if you were the right person for the job) and photo shoots.

Lights, Camera . . . Criticism?

I learned quite quickly that ad agents and photographers have no problem telling you if they don't like your appearance. "We're searching for someone with a different look." Or "The end of your nose is too rounded." Or "We don't like the way your neck curves." Or "Your teeth are too big." Really, nothing is off-limits for these people!

After a while, I noticed I started to be unsure of myself. It seemed my confidence was slipping away. Questions surfaced. Is this shirt right for me? Is my rear getting big? Does my makeup look good? Is my hair hip enough? Why would anyone want to hire me? Should I get this mole on my cheek removed? Do I have enough money for breast implants?

Even though in the short time I'd been in New York I'd landed a national commercial, been on several smaller magazine covers, and appeared in some catalogs, it wasn't enough to offset the negative comments and the comparisons. My sensitive nature soaked them right in. I felt that almost everything about me was wrong. Inadequate. Not good enough.

What Was God Up To?

At the same time, God was using my modeling experience to show me that he had a different plan for my life, a plan that would amount to more than just having my smiling face promoting a product or gracing a magazine cover. This was something that would be much bigger than being a supermodel or an A-list actress. It would be a plan that would have heart—his heart!

It was time to move home.

Yet it seemed to be the worst possible timing. I had just finished my composite card, and I was about to be officially introduced to the market in the Wilhelmina head book.

My roommates thought I was delirious.

"What could be more important than attaining superstar status or making some big bucks?" they argued. "Besides, you're signed with a great agency, you're working with a famous acting coach, and your vocal trainer's the best." They almost had me convinced. But as I watched one light up a joint, one mix a drink, and one pop her birth control pill, it just confirmed my inner conviction that God had something better for me.

A *Real* B.A.B.E.!

The second week after I moved home, I was handed information about a one-year Bible training program. I knew it was for me. Though I'd been a believer since I was young, I'd never really studied God's Word. In fact, I didn't get my first Bible until I was sixteen. Since my future was going to be about God's plans for me, knowing his Word was core. Yet little did I know that this would change my life most dramatically.

As I studied the Bible, I discovered many verses that explained God's view and opinion of me. I found out he created and designed me in a way that delighted him. To him, I was **beautiful**. I learned that I didn't have to look or act perfect for him to love me. He **accepted** me. And he gave me talents and spiritual gifts that he wanted me to develop so I could use them to serve him. I am **blessed** by him. And about that plan I mentioned earlier, it was starting to play out before my eyes. No flashy stuff that was here today and gone tomorrow. God's plan for me is **eternally significant**. From God's perfect perspective, I was a B.A.B.E.—not a sexy, flirty chick in a short skirt and a low-cut top who wanted all the guys to like her, but a *real* B.A.B.E.: beautiful, accepted, blessed, eternally significant! And it's *his* perspective and opinion that matter!

See, he had to heal my self-esteem with the truth of his Word before he could use me to help heal yours. Many of the experiences God has taken me through have been part of his preparation to bring me to this point right now.

For Such a Time as This

These truths have lived in my heart for years, but God has brought them together under the acronym B.A.B.E. for such a time as this. My friend, I have seen teen girls struggle with depression, eating disorders, cutting, alcohol and drug addiction, casual sex, and hopelessness. I believe these are all symptoms of low self-esteem. They're holding many young women back from becoming all God has meant for them to be.

Well, not anymore.

Life will change when you finally see yourself the way God sees you. It's my life mission to help teen girls (and women) get a new perspective on life, on themselves, on God. I'm so blessed to be able to invest my life in the lives of God's girls through writing, speaking, and mission trips.

To every person who reads this, you are a B.A.B.E.! I prove it to you in the first book of the B.A.B.E. Book series, *Girlfriend, You Are a B.A.B.E.!* It's not based on feelings or social standards. It's based on the unchanging truth in God's Word.

(So if you don't have a copy of the book, order one today right off my website at www.andreastephens.com or from the publisher at www.revellbooks.com and get started!)

Oh, by the way. God calls us to imitate Jesus. So I am (and so are you) a model! Just a different kind. Isn't God cool?

WHaT IS a B.A.B.E.?

Get a new view of you! We're putting a spiritual spin on the word "babe" and giving you a scriptural definition of what it really means to be beautiful, accepted, blessed, and eternally significant—a B.A.B.E.! Check it out.

B Is for Beautiful!

You're a divine diva! You're fearfully and wonderfully made—created by God himself! You're a work of art and were not haphazardly thrown together! You were in God's care before you were even born! You were his idea! God thinks you're outrageously gorgeous! God sends his Spirit to live within you to make you beautiful on the inside. You have God-Beauty!

A Is for Accepted!

You're unconditionally loved and accepted by God! You've already won his approval! He's your audience of One! He stands to applaud you because he's proud of you! You belong to God! You're forgiven. You don't need to seek the acceptance of others—you're number one with God. He thinks you rock! Ultimately, what God thinks is all that matters!

B Is for Blessed!

You're the privileged recipient of so many blessings straight from the heart of God! You have blessings no one can take away from you. You have special abilities—tons of talents! As a child of God, you're showered with spiritual blessings like salvation, forgiveness, eternal life, the Holy Spirit, and grace! You've been given spiritual gifts like leadership or encouragement or service! You're so blessed!

E Is for Eternally Significant!

You're here *on* purpose and *for* a purpose! God has a plan for your life! A plan that will bring you true meaning, fulfillment, and satisfaction! A plan that will put to use your special abilities and your spiritual gifts. A plan that will make a difference in the lives of others and in the kingdom of God. It's an eternally significant plan! You matter!

Girlfriend, you are a B.A.B.E.!

1

LEARNING TO LOVE YOUR LOOK

I remember emerging from the subway station, having just met with a photographer and now headed to an acting lesson, when I passed by one of the zillion magazine racks in New York City. I stopped, spun back, and zeroed in on the cover that had caught my eye.

Kari. On the cover of *Seventeen*. *Why didn't I make that cover? What did she have that I didn't?*

In a millimeter of a second, answers flashed in.

Thick straight hair. Creamy beige skin. Bouncy boobs. A flirty look in her aqua-blue eyes. A confidence that made people take notice.

I stopped the thoughts there, breaking in with, *If I looked more like her, maybe it would be my face people saw on that cover.*

Those were my thoughts as a teen. I was wrapped up in wanting to do, to be, to have. I compared myself to everyone else and the modeling industry compared me to everyone else. It bashed my self-image, leaving my self-esteem splattered on the sidewalks of "the city that never sleeps."

And then God stepped in. Now I understand the dangers of wishing I looked like someone else. Now I understand the drain of trying to be what others want me to be. Now I realize that *real* beauty is not about looks. Now I know what is true about me, based on God's unchanging Word. And I want you to know what's true about you too. (Check out Extra Stuff 2 on p. 176.)

GlamTip: How does God define beauty? It's not about being fat free or pimple free; it's about being jealousy free, grudge free, anger free, and selfishness free.

If Only I Looked Like Her

There's a studio I want you to see. Pardon the mess. Artists aren't too particular about their surroundings. I mean, take a glance at this place—little pieces of dry clay stuck to the dusty floor; bags of solid clay leaning against the wall, awaiting their transformation; musty, heavy plastic lining shelves that are perfect drying spots for finished pottery; a messy, moist residue lingering on the steel wheel where the potter works.

And feel the atmosphere! Cool, not cold. (Warmth dries out the clay.) Notice the clay's unusual, earthy smell that hangs in the air?

Oh, look! The potter's about to begin a new piece. Amazing. He throws the clay on the wheel, centering it perfectly. He takes his water-dipped hands and begins to mold the shape he sees on the sketchbook of his mind. His fingers reach into the pot and gently widen the middle of his creation. Both hands move to the outside of the pot and slowly press inward, narrowing the top of the piece. So purposeful! So artistic!

Once the piece has had some drying time, the artist returns. The clay has to have the right amount of firmness for the potter to add the final touches. Selecting the right tool, he adds to the distinction of his current creation. Check out the

ANDREA'S ADVICE

Comparing yourself to others leads only to conceit or contempt toward yourself. Neither is healthy or right. Save yourself some grief—don't compare. U B U!

wavy lines the jagged-edged tool makes. Notice the pattern produced when he presses the wooden stamp onto the clay.

Fascinating. Of course, the greatest tool the artist has is his imagination. Only he can stare at a gray lump of clay while picturing the finished product in his mind.

Hey, look. The potter is smiling. The piece is complete and perfect in his eyes. A unique expression of himself. Truly his work of art.

Want to know what the Old Testament prophet Isaiah said about the potter and the clay?

> O Lord, You are our Father; we are the clay, and You our potter, and we all are the work of Your hand.
>
> Isaiah 64:8 AMP

Just like the potter who handcrafts each piece of pottery, so God has crafted you. He has designed you with great care. He has molded you with his loving hands into the shape that pleases his eye and fills his heart with pride. He is *not* a frustrated artist! He is a skillful artist who knew exactly what he was doing. When he looks at you he sees beautiful! He doesn't have a rating system—we are equally gorgeous to him!

If you choose to believe this truth, then you'll be on your way to loving your look instead of wishing you looked like someone else. **Key words**: choose and truth.

See, you have to decide what you are going to believe about yourself. I had to make that choice many years ago in New York when God began to teach me the *real* meaning of the word *beauty* (get the full story in chapter 11, "Breathtaking Beauty"). Are you going to believe that you're beautifully created? Or will you allow yourself to look at everyone else and think, *If only I had her legs or her lashes or her rear*? That

Want your *real* beauty to show? Choose to make God your sole audience, your audience of One! Live for him, not your peers. This will set you free on the inside, and the *real* you—with your *real* beauty—will show!

will get you nowhere, except discouraged to the point of trying to change stuff about yourself—ultimately a dead-end street.

Glam Tip: It's a proven fact that girls who are into fashion magazines feel worse about their physical appearance than the girls who aren't. Give it some thought.

What "Look" Makes You Beautiful?

Those who live and breathe industries like modeling, dance, and entertainment as well as sports like gymnastics, figure skating, and track are pressed hard to maintain a certain look, a certain body shape, a certain weight. And looking at many of them has caused many of us to try to attain the same standards.

Not possible. Do you have time to work out five hours a day? Has God given you the genetic makeup to match their body types? Your thinking becomes warped when you get your eyes off the fact that God is your potter and you are not supposed to look like someone else.

God has given you a body. That's no news flash. Because he wanted us so individual, no two bods are exactly alike. However, we humans have lumped bodies into three main categories: endomorphs (large bones), mesomorphs (medium-sized bones), and ectomorphs (small bones). Yet within these basic categories, there are millions of combos. Narrow shoulders with broad hips. Thin arms with thick ankles. Slim calves with large feet. It's

Q: "My ankles are very thick and I hate them so much I cry myself to sleep. That sounds trite, but I get really upset about them. As a cheerleader I'm quite self-conscious. Are there any exercises I can do?"

A: Ankle size is generally based on your bone size, not on your fat percentage. You can't change the size of your bones. That's a God-thing. Naturally you can avoid things that draw attention to your ankle area like anklet socks, ankle bracelets, capris, or long skirts that stop at the ankle. Your real challenge is to change the way you look at your ankles. First, are they a family trademark? If so, embrace them. It's one little way God links us to our families. Second, is it possible that your bone size gives you stability so that you can do well as a cheerleader? You need that balance! So look to the positive things, and as my mom always told me, "Just be thankful you have ankles!"

The Perfect Body

The perfect body is tall. It is lean. It is a combination of firmness and fat. It has moles and large knuckles. It has stubborn hair that won't hold a curl.

The perfect body is soft. It is curvy. It is speckled with freckles. It has a nose that is wide. It has pale lips. Its second toe is longer than the first.

The perfect body is large boned. It is strong. It has oily skin and many blackheads. It has slim ankles that wear heels well. It has a rounded stomach.

The perfect body has small breasts. It has dry skin and few blemishes. It has delicate fingers with nails that rarely break. It has full hips.

The perfect body is the one you are in right now; it is a gift from God. It is yours to use as you fulfill God's purposes for you in this life. It is a temple, a sanctuary where the Spirit of its Maker dwells. It is a tent, a temporary home that will pass away. But your soul, your spirit, is the real you. It will last for all of eternity. It is forever.

That's perfect.

whatever God molded for you! There are no right or wrong body types. Every body is constructed just the way God planned.

So what look makes *you* beautiful? The one you already have!

Embrace the Incomparable You!

If girls compare their bods to others and decide to launch an all-out war to try to change themselves (hair color and eye color, fake lashes, nails, and breasts) or reshape themselves (attack those hips, thighs, and buttocks), they will soon find out that no amount of diet or exercise can change their basic look or body type.

Okay, adding blond highlights or getting nail tips is not earth-shaking. But the body issue is! Girls who obsess and insist on change may open themselves up to a full-blown eating disorder. Others fall prey to dabbling in dangerous practices. Think about these:

> Have you ever heard the girl in the stall next to you at school or at a party throwing up her food?
> Are you aware of girls who are *always* running to the bathroom?
> Do you know girls who carry laxatives in their purses?
> Do you know of girls who skip breakfast and lunch but drink coffee or sugary caffeine colas all day to try to stay alert?
> Have you met girls who constantly smoke or chew gum to keep themselves from eating?
> Have you noticed anyone who is always at the gym, trying to burn off calories?
> Do you know girls who take diuretics (water pills) to force their bodies to secrete larger amounts of urine in hopes of dropping a pound or two?

If you or a friend are playing in the danger zone, thinking you'll drop a few harmless pounds, it's time to sound an alarm! Experimenting with vomiting, diuretics, laxatives, compulsive exercise, and drastic dieting can be life threatening. Pardon me for getting technical for a moment, but this stuff is serious.

The dangers of vomiting. Did you know that stomach acid is strong enough to eat your skin and remove tooth enamel? Consistent vomiting forces stomach acid into your esophagus (throat), causing pain, swelling, tearing, and scar tissue, therefore making swallowing difficult.

The dangers of diuretics. Diuretics, more commonly known as "water pills," cause the kidneys to pump out larger-than-normal amounts of urine, forcing out needed fluids and minerals. This in turn causes dehydration and electrolyte imbalance that can cause heart failure.

The dangers of laxatives. Laxatives are those tiny tablets that cause gas pains, abdominal cramps, major bowel movements, diarrhea, water loss, dehydration, and constipation (if the body becomes addicted to them). Laxatives totally disrupt the body, affecting one's normal electrical circuit. This puts the respiratory system and the heart at risk.

The dangers of compulsive exercise. When a girl insists on attempting to burn off every calorie she consumes, or she willingly puts her entire life on hold until her workout is complete, she's suffering from compulsive exercise. Exhaustion, overworked muscles, and an inability to maintain a healthy weight may result. Plus, she misses out on a lot of life outside the gym!

The dangers of drastic dieting. Dressing for prom night or an important date or weighing in for a sport often influence teens to turn to drastic dieting tactics. Is it okay to starve oneself for a short period of time? Perhaps the mega-headaches, fainting spells, and easily caught cold or flu that result will clue you in.

The dangers of compulsive overeating. The pressures to fit cultural standards can result in an opposite reaction in which the person copes by eating, eating, eating. This leads to obesity, which is hard on the heart, the joints, and the ability to get into life.

God has designed the body to work according to a delicate balance. Vomiting, diuretics, laxatives, compulsive exercise, drastic dieting, and compulsive overeating all mess up this balance, putting your body at risk.

Where are *you* with all of this? Are you playing in any danger zones? Many girls don't admit or see the problem until they have a full-blown eating disorder like anorexia (self-starvation) or bulimia (forced vomiting), which can lead to permanent health problems. If you—or someone you know—are exhibiting two or more signs, it's time to **get help**. Talk with a trusted adult or your doctor.

Your Creator God has placed his stamp of approval on you. You are totally accepted by him. Close your eyes and envision him giving you a holy thumbs-up!

Help is always available by calling Remuda Ranch, a treatment center for teens, at 1-800-445-1900. Ask to speak to a counselor or go to www.remuda-ranch.com. You can also contact Eating Disorder Awareness and Prevention at www.edap.org.

I know the pressures get tough. But we've established the fact that comparing yourself is not the way to go. So what are your options? Well, you could just decide you are mediocre, which leads to a blasé and mundane life. Boring. Uneventful. Why try; you won't make it anyway.

Or you can opt to accept the beautiful *you* that God has created and celebrate the unique abilities, talents, and spiritual gifts (check out Extra Stuff 1) that your heavenly Father has given you. You can focus on the cool truths about you as a child of God that are found in the unchanging Bible (see Extra Stuff 2). You can get prepared and pumped up about the God-selected adventures and assignments with your name on them.

Stop right now and pray about it. Jot a note to God telling him what you have decided and why: _____

_____

_____

_____

Q: "Sometimes I wonder if I care too much about the way I look. Where's the line between taking care of myself and caring too much?"

A: That's a very insightful question! The line might be different for each of us, but generally speaking, when a girl thinks about her looks to the point of allowing it to control her actions (she can't leave for school until she looks "perfect" or doesn't show up at something because she's got a zit) or her moods (she gets depressed over a bad hair day or a wrinkled outfit), then the line has been crossed.

If you can get ready to go somewhere, then walk out the door and basically forget about your look, that's good. If you find yourself constantly checking the mirror or your reflection in store windows, fiddling with your hair, and totally primping, it's too much. And if you continually worry about what others may be thinking about your looks, you definitely care too much!

Feeling Beautiful All Under

I'm going to be straight with you. We all have a layer of fat between our skin and our muscles. And as the body matures into womanhood, that fat layer increases. It's normal. It's part of God's design for us to gain weight in the hip and bust area. Why? To begin to prepare the body for

Love Your Look at a Glance

Don't compare your look to others.

See someone's lips, fingers, or legs you'd like to own? Freeze! Instantly thank God for giving her those features. Then thank God for giving you the ones you have.

Eliminate scheming thoughts of ways to change your physical appearance.

Daily praise God for your unique, individual look instead of dogging him with comments like, "Could you have done better than this? Why do I have a nose (or whatever) like this?" Do a 180!

Guard your heart against mean comments by others. Instantly say to yourself, "I forgive you for being an inconsiderate and immature person with your own issues. Lord, teach him/her to be more sensitive to others." God wants us to pray for our enemies, remember?

Select makeup, hairstyles, fashions, and accessories that you feel great wearing.

the childbearing years (when you're married and allowed to have sex—until then, abstinence rules).

One of the things I see girls do is wear things so tight that they make themselves *feel* like an overweight pudge! That's not normal. Obsessing over size to the point of squeezing the bod into something too small—not a good look and not a good feeling.

Case in point: the bra. The number indicates the size of the band or the rib cage (under the bust area), like 34 or 40. The letter indicates the cup size needed to sufficiently hold and cover the breasts, like A or D. The bra size a girl wears is not a reflection of her personal value. But when she buys into the thinking that a lower number and a higher cup letter is the main determinant of her worth, she buys the wrong size. If a girl needs a 38 but straps herself into a 34, what happens? The bra pinches into

ANDREA'S ADVICE

Stay tight with God and you'll continually see what you were made to do; you'll see God's eternally significant plan for your life. Then you'll find true success and true meaning in your time on planet earth! This will give you a beautiful look that is *real*!

her flesh and creates "bra overhang." A bulge. If she buys the 38, good-bye overhang.

The same is true with undies. Today's underwear are not your granny's panties. We are talking barely there. But again, a size 12 versus a size 6 does not make one person better than another. Get what fits.

Let's not overlook low-rise trousers and jeans. The same thing happens. Squeeze the body mid-hip and the flesh is forced upward. It looks like a fat roll. Just buy the right size—or don't wear the pants so low. Why create rolls that otherwise are not there? Crazy!

Don't create your own grief. Wear what fits. Love your body.

Now that you're on your way to loving your look, consider this: every morning the sun comes up and presents you with a brand-new day. It's a new opportunity to present yourself to the world! Well, okay, maybe not to the *whole* world, but at least to your family, friends, classmates, teammates, employer, and other people around you. And most importantly, you get to represent Jesus to others. You are his ambassador representing heaven (your real homeland) to the peeps you come into contact with every day. In order to help you put your best self forward, I've loaded the upcoming chapters with some awesome advice and important info. These tips will get you stepping out in the right direction!

Q: "My parents are constantly ragging on me about getting enough sleep. It's hard to do when I have a ton of homework (okay, I spend a little time on IM). Is it really necessary?"

A: Without a doubt! Sleep is key for looking and feeling your best. Take your appearance. Getting enough sleep chases away puffy eyes, dark circles, sallow skin, and sparkle-less eyes. Packing in your z's also allows your body to recharge and repair. Everyone needs that.

Now about feeling your best. Lack of shut-eye can drag you down, contribute to depression, and make you edgy, all of which will affect your grades and your relationships. Sleep is a brain booster. So you tell me—is it really necessary?

Tough time falling asleep? Help your brain relax by writing down all your frantic thoughts. Keep a flashlight, pad, and pen by your bed. You won't have to remember anything in the morning—it's all on the pad! Plus, read your Bible. God says that he will cause you to be at peace when your mind stays on him (see Isaiah 26:3).

2

savvy skin care

Before you start washing, scrubbing, or lavishing your skin with lotion, you need to know which products to use. To do that, identify your skin type!

The Skin Type Test

Do this simple evaluation:

1. Before you turn out the lights and call it a night, cleanse your face. Do not apply anything to your skin (no astringent or lotion).
2. The next day as soon as you wake up, lay a piece of tissue paper over your entire face. Press the tissue against your forehead, cheeks, sides of your nose, and middle of your chin.
3. Lift the tissue, holding it up to the light. What do you see?
   _____ a. a slight bit of oil
   _____ b. practically no oil

_____ c. lots of oil

_____ d. some oil in some spots

4. Next, go nose-to-nose with a mirror. What do you see?

_____ a. medium-sized pores

_____ b. very small pores

_____ c. large pores

_____ d. medium to large pores in the nose and chin area, otherwise small

5. How often do pimples pop out?

_____ a. occasionally—usually with my period

_____ b. almost never

_____ c. practically always

_____ d. they come and go most of the time

Draw your conclusion:

a = normal skin

b = dry skin

c = oily skin

d = combination skin

Q: "I live where the humidity is high almost year-round, and my skin constantly feels oily. I hate how it shines at school. I use an oil-free moisturizer, but it's not totally effective. Help!"

A: Get yourself some oil-absorbing products. First, shine-free powder (look for the cool blue). Apply a light dusting and it will be adios shine (and even redness). Keep it in your purse to reapply for anytime shine. Second, if you don't like the powder principle, try the oil-absorbing sheets. Use them to blot away excess oil almost instantly. Plus, they can soak up unwanted oil without messing up your makeup. Tuck these silky smooth sheets in your backpack! They're available at most beauty supply stores.

The Best Match

It's frustrating, confusing, and downright maddening. Pacing the aisles and scanning the product choices is overwhelming. How are you supposed to know what's best for you? By carefully reading labels and choosing products that match your skin type. Otherwise you will not get good results. For instance, products for dry skin contain extra emollients (oil) to moisturize the skin. If you already have oily skin, applying this product will make it worse.

Open the cosmetic bag of the average teen and you will see a hodgepodge of stuff. A mix of Neutrogena, L'Oréal, Clinique, Cover Girl, and more! Individually these products may be good, but you'll be lessening their full potential by not using them with the other products from the same line. It's best to use all skin-care products from the same company since they have been formulated to work together. So if you switch, make it a total change! (On the flip side, when it comes to glam makeup, the most important thing is the color, not the company).

Look for allergy-tested, fragrance-free, non-comedogenic (won't clog pores, which creates blackheads), pH balanced (balanced alkaline and acidic levels) brands that have been stripped of ingredients that cause redness, rashes, breakouts, burning, or itching.

Love the Skin You're In

Your skin is totally dependent upon the person wearing it—you! You know your skin type. You know which products to select. But why bother? Why spend time (and cash) on your skin? Well, let me give you a quick rundown on this awesome stuff that covers your bones, tendons, muscles, veins, and life-giving organs.

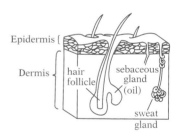

It perspires, which cleanses your bod of harmful toxins. It regulates your body temp at 98.6 degrees. It produces vitamin D when you're in the sunshine. It allows you to blush. It has two layers—the epidermis (top) and the dermis (bottom). It contains pores, sweat glands, blood vessels, oil glands, hair follicles, and tough elastin fibers that keep it young looking. It sheds. It creates a new layer of cells every forty-eight hours. It burns. It contains melanin that causes it to tan. And the coolest characteristic of all—it is sensitive to touch.

Sure, it might break out, peel if you burn it, or scar from acne (this can be success-

Do you have an oily T-zone? Yep, that's across the forehead and down the center of the face!

fully removed with laser treatment), but it's still an incredible body covering that God has given you. The time and cash you spend on its care will be worth the investment. Love it, lavish it with TLC. Here's how.

Squeaky Clean

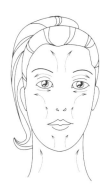

Keeping your skin fresh and clean requires double duty—once in the morning, once in the evening. Choose a cleansing bar, lotion, or gel that is detergent free and fragrance free. Work it into a sudsy lather while moving your fingertips in a circular motion. Your facial skin and muscles are very delicate, so avoid pulling, rubbing, or pressing hard! Rinse off the cleanser using lukewarm water; then gently pat dry with a clean towel.

Speaking of clean skin, take a daily shower or bath—especially after a workout and always during your period. Follow up with body lotion and deodorant.

Glam Tip: Never go to bed with your makeup on! Never go to bed with your makeup on! Never go to bed with your makeup on!

Q: "I recently went through a growth spurt that left stretch marks on my knees, hips, and breasts. They make me feel embarrassed. What should I do?"

A: That's a question women of all ages ask! Stretch marks, which are breaks in the collagen fiber beneath the skin's surface, can be caused by growth spurts, pregnancy, or rapid weight gain. I recommend trying vitamin E oil. There are also several creams designed for pregnant women that can help restore elasticity to the skin.

Rub the oil directly into the affected areas. Keep in mind that the visibility of stretch marks often fades over time. My best advice to you is to not allow these harmless lines to hurt your self-image! There is no such thing as an ideal body, but there is a thing called real life. This is just part of it! But it is nothing that will keep you from becoming the very best you. Stretch marks are surface. Who you are is much deeper than that!

Natural Additions

Sage, avocado, rosemary. Sounds like a bad salad, huh? Before you toss it out, give God some credit. He brilliantly designed nature with nutrients and special properties that can benefit our skin! Extracted from certain flowers, herbs, grasses, fruits, roots, and trees, these beautifying ingredients are turned into liquid or oil form and infused into some great products. Here's a quick rundown on the purpose of these special ingredients so you can determine which your skin needs.

To soothe: rose water, chamomile, cucumber, aloe vera, witch hazel

To moisturize: avocado, wheat germ, apricot, geranium, rosewood, chamomile, marigold

To reduce oil: juniper, lemon, bergamot, rosemary, lavender, clary sage

To fight acne: tea tree, lavender, bergamot, geranium, myrrh, myrtle, thyme, rosemary, aloe vera.

Tune Up with Toner

Girls are always stumped during the Sensational Skin Care Quiz I give at The B.A.B.E. Seminar™ when I ask if a toner (or astringent) can clog pores. The answer is **no**! A toner removes excess dirt, oil, or soap residue from the epidermis (the top layer of skin). Some even chemically exfoliate the skin, removing the dead cells that can leave a dull look to your appearance if not frequently sloughed off. It also causes the edges of pores to swell, making them appear smaller. Dab some astringent or toner on a fluffy 100 percent cotton ball and apply it to your face using circular motions—avoid your eye area.

So, here we go. (Pretend you're at The B.A.B.E. Seminar™.) True or False: toner or astringent can clog pores.

ANDREA'S ADVICE

Keep your focus on Jesus's beauty and seek to be like him! "One thing I ask of the LORD, this is what I seek: that I may dwell in the house of the LORD all the days of my life, to gaze upon the *beauty* of the LORD and to seek him in his temple" (Psalm 27:4 NIV, emphasis added).

Moisturize Magic

Make your skin feel good all over! Treat it to the soft, smoothing effects of moisturizer. This will seal in natural fluids and replace moisture your skin loses due to sun, wind, perspiration, artificial air conditioning and heating, and pollution. All skin types need moisture! Normal to dry skin can use a heavy moisturizer; normal to oily skin can go with an oil-free type.

Glam Tip: Use specially formulated eye cream at night, always applying it with your ring finger—the one with the lightest touch!

Ten TLC Tips

1. Pamper your skin from the inside out by drinking six to eight glasses of water every day. Sodas, chai, and lattes don't count! Pure H_2O, girl! This flushes and hydrates your system, which is key for healthy-looking skin.

2. Don't want skin cancer? Don't want extra wrinkles? Don't want dark spots? Then act *now* by protecting your precious skin *every day* from the sun's harmful rays! Apply sunscreen—SPF 15 or higher. Smooth it on your face right after your moisturizer, or use a moisturizer or foundation that already has sunscreen. Rub some into the back of your hands to minimize future age spots. Use extra on your bod (especially between 10 a.m. and 2 p.m.) when you'll be outside for sports or a day at the beach.

To get a healthy golden glow, apply a sunless tanning lotion or foam—it's a tan in a can, but it's still better than harmful UVB and UVA-1 rays. Experiment to find the lotion that mixes best with your natural oils (some can turn orangish). Apply in a circular motion, watching to be sure you don't miss a spot. Finished? Wash your palms ASAP. Spray booths can do all this for you too. They sorta work like a car wash—strip down, step in, spray, turn around, spray back side, step out, wipe off!

3. Steam clean. Once or twice a week, open your pores by placing your face over a bowl of steaming water (or press a wet, warm

washcloth against your face) for two to four minutes. Then splash your face with warm water about ten times. Follow with toner and moisturizer.

4. Chase away dead skin. Every other day a new layer of skin cells is produced in your dermis. As they move up through the epidermis, they lose fluid, flatten out, and die! So twice a week, use a facial scrub to chase away dead, dull-looking skin cells from your skin's surface. Choose a product made with tiny round beads. Gently work in circular motion. Rinse well.

5. Got acne? Clear it up, don't cover it up! Acne attacks occur when a blackhead or whitehead gets infected. Switch to a cleanser or toner that contains salicylic acid. Then apply a product with benzoyl peroxide directly to zits to kill bacteria and speed up the healing process. If these over-the-counter zit zappers aren't giving you the results you want, go to your local dermatologist, who can prescribe a topical antibiotic, Retin-A, or powerful Accutane. All acne can be treated!

Glam Tip: Don't squeeze your zits! Steam or apply a wet, warm washcloth to them every night to speed up the maturation process. Yes, they have to form first. When white pus appears at the top, steam, then *gently* use the pads of your fingers (not your nails) to press straight down to the sides of the pimple. Don't squeeze, just press down (squeezing can cause pus to spread, thus creating *more* pimples). If the infected matter does not come out, it's not ready. Apply medicated product and wait until tomorrow.

6. Lip neglect? Chapped, cracked lips are evidence. Lips don't have sweat glands and natural oils, so it's you or nothing! Glide on some medicated lip balm to heal, soften, and prevent chapping. Hey, you can even choose one in your favorite flavor like cherry, wild berry, or orange! Keep the balm handy in your purse, car, and backpack.

7. Dastardly black dots? Pesky blackheads are a mixture of dead skin cells, oil, and bacteria that build up

Did you know Esther spent a whole year having special skin treatments before she was taken to meet King Xerxes? Get her entire story in *Bible B.A.B.E.s: The Inside Dish on Divine Divas*.

Beauty Bonus with Natalie Grant: "I love Cetaphil. It's a good, all-around product that is great for my skin. It even helps with acne. Plus, I always wear sunscreen! I wish I had not worshipped the sun when I was younger because I don't like the effects I'm seeing now."

inside our pores, especially on our chins and noses. They are hard to eliminate, but you can temporarily exterminate them using a comedone extractor—a small tool with a tiny hole on the end. First, open your pores by putting a warm, wet washcloth on your face for a few minutes. Then, using the extractor, encircle the blackhead and press straight down. The blackhead—oil and all—will ooze up out of the pore. Extractors are available at beauty supply stores.

Q: "I messed up waxing my upper lip hair, and now I have little scabs in the places where my skin got pulled off along with my lip hair. Yuck! What did I do wrong?"

A: Ouch! I did the same thing my first few attempts at waxing my lip hair! I even have a little scar from it! I have since learned to apply powder to the area before applying the hot wax. That usually keeps the wax from sticking to your skin. Plus, waxing is more successful when you allow the hair to grow back in before attempting to wax again—that gives the wax more hair to adhere to. While it is growing in, use Jolene Crème Bleach to get it light toned. Naturally, the best thing to do is go to a salon to have lip hair zipped away. They are more experienced!

Q: "How can I make my teeth whiter?"

A: First, brush twice a day for two weeks with baking soda—yep, the stuff right out of the pantry! It's tough on stains caused by cola, coffee, and tea. Then add a whitening pre-brush rinse—it's like a sixty-second bubble bath for your mouth. Still stained? Try the whitening strips from the drugstore (medium strength) or the dentist (professional strength). After that, the most effective whitening is done professionally with whitening gel and light. Pricey but powerful!

8. Vital vitamins! Take a multiple vitamin daily and some extra vitamin A, E, and C—the skin, hair, and nail vitamins. Look for zinc to help with acne. Vitamins from a whole food source are my favorites. Get more vitamin info at www.puritan.com.

9. Facial hair? Moustaches on females are just not right! Nonetheless, out from the skin grows hair and some of it lands on your upper lip. Yikes! Get rid of it! Cream bleach lightens noticeably dark hair. Plucking is okay if you have a few strays. Waxing works to zip it off for a week or two. Shaving—don't go there. Electrolysis is exact and rids you of the hair if you can stand the zap from the tiny needle that slips into the hair follicle. Laser light destroys the follicle yet is costly. Take your pick and good luck.

10. Heavenly heels! Pay attention to the skin on your feet—especially heels! Without constant care, they get rough, dry, cracked, and calloused. Not pretty! Soak them in warm water for ten minutes, then scrub them with a pumice paddle (it has a rock-like appearance). At bedtime, slather on a special foot cream that contains conditioning oils. Your feet will thank you.

ANDREA'S ADVICE

Refresh dry, dull-looking skin with this facial mask made from fresh, natural ingredients. Here's the very simple recipe:

$\frac{1}{2}$ cup of plain yogurt

5 fresh strawberries

Mash the strawberries using the back of a fork, then add them to the yogurt. Blend well. Apply the mixture to your face. Wait for ten minutes. (Use this time to lie down, relax, catch up on your devotions, memorize a Bible verse, or boost your boy info by reading *Boyland: A B.A.B.E.'s™ Guide to Understanding Guys*.) Rinse the yogurt mixture off with lukewarm water.

So what does this do? The lactic acid in the yogurt works to get rid of dry, dead skin cells (not to mention the yogurt provides protein and calcium), and the acidic nature of the berries (and burst of vitamin C) leaves the skin feeling happy and refreshed! Good-bye dry-leather look!

Check out more homemade beauty concoctions at www .andreastephens.com (Hot Topics: Look and Feel Beautiful).

3

Makeup Mania

During my modeling days in NYC, I had the luxury of working with talented makeup artists, so I've collected quite a few tips and tricks of the trade. Did you know that when models are out of the limelight, they wear very little makeup? They give their skin a chance to breathe. They want a natural look—and that's what I'm going to give you! No trendy extremes for the real supermodels. So here are the "barely there" makeover techniques that work for them and will work for you.

Hiding or Highlighting Your Look?

What's the purpose of painting this gooey stuff on? Why even bother with cosmetics? To hide behind or try to alter your facial features? Because you want to make a statement by using wild colors? Because you think it will make you attractive to a certain guy? To make yourself look or feel more grown-up? **These aren't good reasons for wearing makeup.** Wear it to highlight your beautiful God-given features! You are already gorgeous to God—no altering needed. There is no ideal face shape that you need to copy. And the truth about guys and makeup? They really don't like it and would rather see the natural you. Go for a touch of gloss to make your smile shine; use a bit of soft liner to accentuate the warmth in your eyes—you get the picture. To emphasize the reason for wearing makeup, identify its purpose. Know what each technique does, then choose if it's for you!

The Natural Look

It is *hugely* important that your makeup colors match up with your skin's undertone—either cool or warm. Skip over to "The Colorful Influence" on page 91 to get the full scoop.

Glam Tip: If you are young, wearing makeup can make you look like you're playing dress up.

Building a Foundation

Like the necessary undercoat an artist lays first on a canvas, foundation (or base) lays the groundwork for the *real* glam look. Foundation evens out your skin tone, giving a unity of color to your face. Foundation also serves as a gentle shield, protecting your skin from wind, dirt, and humidity. It will even give your skin a smoother appearance.

Select a lightweight formula that goes with your skin type (dry, oily, acne prone). Choose the feel you enjoy (liquid, stick, mousse, gel). Match it to your skin tone by dabbing a bit on your jawline. If it blends in and is hardly noticeable, go with it! Use a cosmetic sponge to apply it evenly to your entire face including your eyelids and your lip line, blending at your jawline (not on your neck). Wipe off any excess on eyebrows.

Q: "I don't like to wear foundation in the hot summer weather, yet it looks like something is missing. Help!"

A: Skin highlighters or shimmer sticks are perfect for adding a little glow that brightens up your look. Choose from pinks, soft peach, or bronze.

Purpose: _____

Conceal or Reveal

Teen girls are crazy about concealer or cover sticks. It gives a pinch more coverage to dark under-eye circles and reddish zits. (Don't use it to cover freckles—freckles rock!)

The concealer should be one shade lighter than your foundation. Now's the time to slide a touch of it directly under your bottom lashes, then downward about an inch. Creamy ones are best.

Purpose: _____

Glam Tip: Extend concealer—or a lighter shade of foundation—outward on top of your cheekbone (toward your hairline) to highlight the area. Apply a slightly darker shade of foundation under your cheekbone to create dimension. Blend well. This is especially fun to try on fancy occasions.

Polish with Powder

Follow with a light dusting of translucent (glowing—as if light were coming through) face powder to set the foundation, absorb excess shine, and minimize pore size, giving your skin a polished appearance. Powder also sets the stage for your powdered eye shadow and blushes to be applied with ease. Key word with powder: **light!**

Purpose: _____

If you are skipping foundation, you can still even out your skin tone (though to a lesser degree) by starting with a shade of powder that is *closest* to your skin tone. Use loose powder or pressed powder with a brush (which makes it loose) to avoid the caked (and fake) look sometimes caused by the powder-puff pad! Speaking of the puff pad—get rid of it. Continual use causes bacteria buildup. Obviously, you don't

ANDREA'S ADVICE

Are you wearing makeup? Be consistent! Show the world a similar face each day. Of course, you don't want to become a slave to your shadows and blushes, and there will be times you won't want to wear makeup at all. Still, make an effort to look your best every day.

need a layer of translucent powder on top of the skin-toned powder you just applied!

Skin-Toned Powder Purpose: _____

Choosing to Blush

Blush adds a soft radiance of color to your face, emphasizes your cheekbone area, and centers more attention on your eyes,

making you look alive and fresh. Sweep your blush across your cheeks in an upward movement. Blush should go no further in toward your nose than the center of your eye, and shouldn't extend lower than the bottom of your nose. If you apply blush to your forehead, chin, and neck, be sure you do it very subtly, much lighter than your cheeks. Light- and medium-toned skins can select a neutral tone like mocha pink. Dark-skinned girls can handle a deeper shade like berry or plum. Forget rosy red, hot pink, or burnt brick. The right color will minimize the contrast between your skin tone and blush color and add to a natural look.

Purpose: _____

Glam Tip: Oops! Add too much blush? Rather than trying to wipe it off, simply tone it down by applying a light dusting of translucent face powder over the top!

Q: "I recently saw a blush that came with two different colors in it. One was lighter than the other. What's up with that?"

A: When two colors are offered, you can contour or create depth by using the darker shade right under your cheekbone, then applying the lighter shade directly on your cheekbone. This makes the cheekbone appear more prominent.

Shadowland

Create a bit of depth and interest using shadows. Choose neutral tones with sparkle or a matte finish. First, apply a light shade of eye shadow (perhaps ivory or soft pink) starting from your lashes, then over the lids and up toward your brows. Apply a medium shade on the outer three-fourths of your lids, extending the shadow up into your crease. Blend well.

Purpose: _____

The Defining Moment

Now it's time to define your baby blues, big browns, groovy greens—and everything in between! Using a soft-kohl eye pencil in a color that matches your lashes (brown, brown-black, or charcoal) will give the look of thicker lashes. Apply the liner directly against your lashes, making the outer corners a bit thicker. For a smudged look, line with eye shadow, using the edge of the applicator to get a thin line.

Lining the top only is a contemporary look. Lining top and bottom is a classic look. No lining is totally cool too. Lining too much—not a good look at all! Never line on the inside edge of the eyelid. It's unhealthy and makes the eyes look small.

Purpose: _____

Glam Tip: Shaky hand? Make a row of dots with the liner, connecting them with a sponge-tip or cotton-tip applicator.

All about Lashes

It's mascara time! Using brown or brown-black, coat the tips of your lashes with the tip of the mascara wand. Wait thirty seconds, then

ANDREA'S ADVICE

Take advantage of tester units in stores, but use a bit of caution. Use a tissue to wipe off *all* sample products in the tester unit before you apply them to your face. Then use a clean tissue to apply the blush and a fresh Q-tip for eye shadows. Be safe and sanitary!

coat the entire lashes, working the wand bristles into your lashes for great coverage. To apply mascara to bottom lashes, tip your chin down, looking up into the mirror. Come up underneath lashes. Use an eyelash comb to separate stuck-together lashes. Don't share mascara with others.

Purpose: _____

Glam Tip: False eyelashes are the rage, but why go fake? Just switch to a microfiber mascara that is designed to lengthen and thicken your own lashes. The microfibers in the basecoat attach to your lashes, then the top coat delivers the thickness and color. Marvelous!

Luscious Lips

Finish your look with lovely lips. Have fun with your glosses and lipsticks. For longer-lasting color, use a lip pencil to line along your lips, then fill it in. Top it off with a light- to medium-toned gloss. Long-lasting sticks that stain the lips work wonders too. Steer clear of dark tones that will make lips look small or reds that can make a girl look like she's playing dress up! Lip color will always look better if it's on the lighter side. If you can't find that perfect shade, try mixing two shades together. For some extra pop, put some frosted or super-shiny gloss in the center of your lips.

Lips are the entrance to your mouth. This reminds me of a prayer in Psalms that all of us B.A.B.E.s can pray: "Let the words of my mouth and the meditation of my heart be acceptable in Your sight, O Lord" (Psalm 19:14 AMP).

Purpose: _____

Tweezer Talk

Are you killing your look by committing eyebrow murder? This will definitely help!

Eyebrows should "frame" your eyes. Brows that are too close or that run together like a furry caterpillar above your eyes are as frightening as brows that are too far apart! Neither one achieves your best look.

The basic rule for knowing where brows are to begin is this: measure straight up from the tear duct (inside corner) of each eye, then move a fraction toward center. You can pluck straggly hair growing between brows. Never, however, wax or shave off your entire brow.

Now, let's talk arches! Are you sportin' a brow that is the same thickness from beginning to end? Typically, the start of the brow is the thickest, and then it begins to thin toward the highest peak of the brow, also known as the arch. From there, the brow tapers off to the end. Some brows arch in the center, some a bit farther out.

To locate the top of the arch, simply brush your eyebrows downward using a brow brush or an unused toothbrush. See the highest point? That's the top of your arch. Use that as a guide to know which hairs to pluck. Removing the hairs under the arch area and on the brow bone will visually open the eye by creating more space (which allows for some fun eye shadow options).

Here are a few more brow beautifying tips:

- If shaping your brows has you stumped, a one-time visit to a professional salon will get you started, and then you can maintain the shape at home.
- In preparing to pluck, grasp the hair as close to the root as possible using a sharp pair of slanted tweezers. Pull in one quick motion in the same direction that the hair grows.

ANDREA'S ADVICE

Got mascara on your skin? Don't wipe it off wet. Give it a few seconds to dry, then touch it with a wet Q-tip. Twirl and lift.

Remember that less is best. Let it be your bright eyes and sparkling smile that others notice about you, not your wild eyeliner or lip color!

Beauty Bonus with Tammy Trent: "My biggest insecurity as a teen was my skin. I had it treated with an antibiotic and Accutane. I was lucky not to have any side effects since it's a strong medication. Isn't it comforting to know that God even cares about how we feel when we have a zit?"

Avoid plucking above the brows unless you have a few strays up there doing their own thing.

When plucking, remove hairs one at a time and row by row so as not to get carried away! How thick or how thin your brows become is personal preference; just try to retain the arch. Experimenting can create a slightly different look, but remember that you can't instantly change your mind. You'll have to wait for the hairs to grow back!

Check daily for reappearing strays, tweezing as soon as possible.

If brows are long and curly, brush them upward, then trim them so they lie flat and in the right direction.

Unruly brows can be tamed with clear gel mascara or by applying hair spray to the brow brush and combing through brows.

The best time to tweeze is before your shower or before bedtime. This allows any redness to fade before applying makeup.

If plucking is painful, apply an ice cube or a dab of Baby Orajel to numb the area, thus eliminating the sting of tweezing. Pluck in the direction of your hair growth to avoid extra pain.

When finished, always be sure to check your makeup in natural daylight to see how it looks. All great makeup artists will position the model near a window.

Does your eyebrow need extending? Here's how you can know: stand eight feet away from the mirror and determine if you can see the last third of your eyebrow. If not, use brow powder to slightly extend your eyebrow. Here's a simple rule: line up a pencil from the outer edge of your nostril to the outer edge of your eye. That's about where your eyebrow should end. Fill in with a matching brow powder (pencils get waxy looking) using short, wispy strokes.

A *Real* Model

Now all you need is a friendly smile, because you are a model too! Every day you model Christ to other teens that need to know him. Show them how great it is to have a Savior who wants to bless their lives and get them through the tough stuff of life. Wow! Now that's being a model!

Grab your Bible, flip open to Proverbs 6:16–17, and discover the kind of eyes the Lord hates (yes, hates). What do you express with *your* eyes?

4

HaiR 101

It blows out of place with even the slightest wind, goes limp in humid weather, needs daily attention, can steal more time than it's worth, and curls opposite of the way you planned, creating styles you never dreamed of. So you mousse, you gel, you spritz, you defuse, you flat iron—and it's *still* doing its own thing.

Thus the "I'm having a bad hair day" phrase was coined.

I can't guarantee to eliminate all future hair-gone-wrong days. Neither can I explain every cool cut or styling method—there are *way* too many! My purpose here? Some basic 101 info to arm you with knowledge as you venture out to discover the cuts, colors, techniques, and styles that are *you*!

The Mane Event

Hair, much like skin, is made up of layers. The *cuticle* is the outer layer. It has tiny, scale-like cells that point downward and protect the inner layer. The *cortex*, or inner layer, is a fibrous substance with long cells. Its job is to give elasticity and strength to the hair. The cortex also contains the pigment that gives your hair color. Hidden away in the center of the hair shaft is the *medulla*. The medulla gives the hair strength and thickness. There is little or no medulla in super fine hair but abundant medulla in thick hair. It takes a stretch of your imagination to envision that each single hair has all three of these layers. But they're there and they need to be cared for.

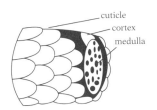
cuticle
cortex
medulla

The amount of wave—or lack of it—in your hair depends on its basic shape. You would need a microscope to see this, but your hair strands fall in one of three shapes: round, oval, or flat.

Round strands produce straight hair; oval strands result in wavy hair; flat strands will leave you with curly hair. You don't necessarily have all the same shape strands throughout your head. It may be curly around your face (flat strands) but nearly straight in the back (round strands). Get to know your hair so you know what you're working with!

Make an X in each column next to the description that fits you.

Type	Texture	Density	Shape
____dry	____fine	____thin	____straight
____oily	____coarse	____thick	____curly
____normal	____medium	____medium	____wavy
____combo	____combo	____combo	____combo

Do you have:

_____ dry scalp (flaky skin)

_____ dandruff (a condition that needs medical attention)

_____ split ends

The Bible says a woman's hair is her glory. It also says we are ambassadors or representatives of Christ. Represent him to others in an appealing, well-groomed way.

Going for Your Personal Best . . . Style!

Before you strut into a salon and plop into the stylist chair, take inventory of the following to help figure out what style is right for you personally!

What's your babe-a-licious face shape? Pull your hair straight back, analyze your face shape, then apply this simple guideline: try not to mimic your face shape with your hairstyle.

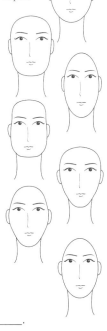

Round beauty. Stay away from a super curly, short style. Go longer, straighter, with volume on top.

Square beauty. Keep your curls or fullness away from the corners of your forehead and jawline.

Oblong beauty. Add fullness at the cheekbone—try long bangs, keep length above shoulder, avoid volume on top.

Pear beauty. Go the opposite of your face shape—volume and lift using waves on top and smoothness near the jawline.

Heart beauty. Save the fullness for your chin area, forget big bangs.

Diamond beauty. Avoid fullness in the cheekbone area.

Oval beauty. No overall oval shape to your hair.

My face shape is _____.

Choose a style that lets you be *you*. Just because it's the latest thing doesn't mean it will look stunning on you.

What's your hair capable of? You can't force your hair to do what it can't! If you have oily, fine, straight hair, a full, wavy look will take forever to achieve! Trust me, you'll be happier with the results if you try styles that work with your hair.

My hair is best when _____.

What's your personality? Bubbly girls usually don't wear long, sophisticated curls or fancy twists. Likewise, shy, reserved girls rarely turn up with hair that is spiked, shaved, or has uneven sides.

My personality is _____.

What's your lifestyle? Active, sporty, or on-the-go glam girls may need a cut that is short and easy to care for or a no-fuss shoulder-length style that can be pulled back out of the way. But if you've got the time and desire, take a shot at a more complicated look.

My lifestyle is _____.

What's in your closet? Match up your hairstyle with your wardrobe. Super-short hair spiked with pomade doesn't fit a closet full of classic-looking clothes. Go with a haircut that does not limit your dressing.

My clothes are _____.

What's your body like? Sound a bit overboard? I'm just being straight with you. Choose a style in proportion with your height and weight. Thick, full hair looks better on a tall girl but would overpower a short, petite girl. A flat, sleek style can make the wide-boned, heavier-set girl appear wider—she needs volume. Are you getting it? (Oh, there's no right or wrong body type, remember?)

My beautiful bod is _____.

What's your budget? Okay, this isn't about the actual style, but it matters. If you go with something like a layered cut with highlights, it will need more attention more often. Do you have the bucks for it?

My budget is about _____.

So, based on this inventory, what can you conclude so far? _____

_____

> **Glam Tip:** Want to speed up your hair growth? Massaging your scalp for five minutes stimulates blood circulation and the oil-producing glands in the skin that nourish the scalp and promote growth. Massaging is also relaxing!

The Basics

Sweet-Smelling Shampoo

Shampooing is the key to clean, shiny, free-moving hair. Squirt about a half-dollar-size drop of shampoo into your palm. Go for a tropical or fruit scent to make the chore more pleasurable. Rub it between your hands and apply it evenly to your wet hair. Use your fingertips to work the shampoo all the way to the roots where hair tends to be oiliest. Massage those bubbles along your hairline and at the nape of your neck.

Next, rinse with warm water while running your fingers through your hair, chasing away the last trace of shampoo. If your hair was super oily to start with, shampoo again.

The shampoo you choose is important, and it's more effective if it matches your hair type (dry, normal, or oily) and your hair texture (fine, medium, or coarse). Look for the pH balance indicator of 4.5 to 6.5 on the label of your shampoo. Many shampoos now have sun-protection ingredients to prevent sun damage.

Spending a few extra bucks on professional hair-care products (as opposed to supermarket types that can be high in detergent and alkali) is worth it. Have the confidence of knowing that the products you're using aren't damaging your locks.

If you need to use a detergent shampoo, store half of it in another container, fill up the original bottle with water, and shake

Beauty Bonus with Rebecca St. James: "I've discovered a shampoo that is perfect for my brunette hair. It picks up my auburn highlights, especially the places that I once had lightened. It's called Tealights Color-Boosting Shampoo with Cherry Bark Tea by Origins."

it vigorously. The half-shampoo, half-water mixture weakens the detergent. It also makes the shampoo last longer.

Glam Tip: Greasy hair looks darker, separates, and is unappealing. Greasy hair can easily be avoided with shampooing every day or every other day. Plus, clean hair responds better to curling and styling.

Cushy Conditioners

Need to smooth those cuticles, fight the frizzies from humid weather, or add moisture? Try a conditioner. Conditioners are available in both deep-penetrating and instant types. Deep-penetrating conditioners work their way into the hair strand to moisturize and nourish. A deep conditioner is supposed to be left on your hair for five to fifteen minutes before you rinse it out. Most deep conditioners work better and penetrate deeper if you wrap your head in a hot, damp towel or sit under a hooded hair dryer for about ten minutes. Use deep conditioners once a month on normal hair. Use more often on colored, damaged, permed, or dry hair—maybe two to three times a month. Oily hair rarely needs a deep conditioner except perhaps after a chemical process such as a perm.

An instant conditioner is applied on hair ends (not roots) when you need it. Instant conditioners actually coat the hair strand with a waxy

Q: "Is it true that lemon juice will lighten my hair, giving me a fun summer look?"

A: Lemon juice, coupled with the sun, has been known to slightly lighten hair a hue or two. But there are no guarantees you'll get the perfect shade or that you'll think it's fun! For instance, a brunette may end up with an orangish tint while a girl with ash-blond hair may get a yellowed look. Perhaps you could just try juicing up a few streaks in the front to try it out. Otherwise, when you squeeze a few drops of that tangy juice on your hair, be ready for anything!

substance, making your hair manageable and tangle free, but they also often make your hair too soft and less curly. Use more or less instant conditioner to suit your own hair. Avoid products with beeswax in them.

Be doubly sure to thoroughly rinse out conditioners using warm water, running your fingers through your hair . . . you know the drill. If cream conditioners prove too heavy for your hair, use a leave-in conditioner—apply to towel-dried hair but don't rinse out.

Glam Tip: Are you a glam girl with swimmer's hair? Say good riddance to that green tint using a rinse made with one tablespoon baking soda dissolved in one cup of warm water, or give your hair a quick rinse with tomato juice to counteract the effects of the chlorine and eliminate that green glow.

Chances are you'll be spending more time in the sun during the summer—pool parties, beach bashes, BBQs, sandpit volleyball games, softball tournaments, family day at the lake, or just going out for a jog. Summer and sun go together. Therefore, after a shampoo, a rinse, and a quick towel dry, spritz your damp hair with a leave-in conditioner that's filled with sun-protection ingredients. Your hair needs a defense plan to keep the ultraviolet light from leaving your hair dry and damaged. Look for an SPF 25 or higher. Also, scout around for special spray-on products to toss in your tote that you can spritz on to absorb harmful rays. There are several hydrating "milks" on the market that contain both SPF and moisture—the perfect blend for summer.

Glam Tip: Want to add some temporary golden rays of sunshine to your hair? Look for beach blonde shimmer gel. Especially great on natural blondes and strawberry redheads, this sparkling, gold-toned gel adds highlights to all shades of hair. Get a streaked look by applying it to selected strands of dry hair. Or apply to wet hair for that sleeked-back look. It's perfect for that poolside party with your best pals.

A Cut Above

You've investigated your hair, taken an eye-opening inventory, and heard the basics on care. Now it's time to talk **cut**! A well-cut head of hair is your foundation for creating the style you want. The quality of the cut affects the way the hair falls, the way it moves, the way it curls, and the way it enhances (or detracts from) your overall look. The goal is to accentuate and frame your beautiful face shape, complement your head shape, and be an expression of who you are ('dos come in sassy, romantic, sporty, practical, trendy, classic—you name it).

Scissor-cut styles leave the ends blunt, which is the way to go for those with thin hair. Razor-cut styles make for a wispier look, especially around the edges or the fringe. Thick hair can handle this. However, some stylists believe the razor is the way to go with *all* cuts. On thick hair it can reduce bulk, and on fine hair it adds texture to create fullness. Overall, the hair lays better with the razor, which should be extremely sharp.

Your hair should be trimmed every six to eight weeks to retain the shape of your hairstyle and prevent split ends. Say good-bye to the split-end saga! Split ends occur when the first two layers of the hair strand—cuticle and cortex—wear away because of hair dryers, curling irons, hot rollers, and other kinds of abuse. This causes the medulla's fine milk-like strands to split. If the ends are not cut off, the split will continue up the hair strand, leaving it thin, frizzed, and weak. No product can solve the split-end problem, though many claim to. Split ends must be cut off regularly.

Q: "I've been using a flat iron to get a straighter look. However, it leaves my hair looking dry, and the tips are frizzy. What can I do to keep this from happening?"

A: First, make sure your hair is completely dry before using the flat iron (I recommend ceramic). Second, be sure the temperature on your flat iron is not too hot (many irons come with adjustable heat). Next, always apply a silicone-based product that will protect your hair from losing all its moisture. Silicone also adds shine and softness and fights the frizzies. Finally, avoid the temptation of holding the flat iron on the tips of your hair. As you are ironing your tresses, move the iron fairly quickly down your hair and right off the ends without stopping. Don't fry the ends!

Note: Don't get brave and use a hair-straightening kit at home. Go to a salon! Too many hair catastrophes happen at home!

Salon Sayings

Don't you hate it when you do your best to describe to your stylist the totally cool cut you're after only to end up with something completely different? Help is on the way! Besides bringing in a photo of the look you like, learn to talk their language! Here's some stuff that will help you feel more confident and able to speak with knowledge to your stylist.

Blunt. Hair is cut so that all the ends, when combed straight down, are even and level with each other, the way a paintbrush is cut.

Beveled. This is slightly similar to a blunt cut, except that the hair either underneath or on top is a tiny bit shorter. This helps the hair bend under or look fuller on short styles.

Layered. Hair is cut so it will fluff and have more fullness. It's shorter on top, creating more fullness there, and gradually achieves more length in the back.

Tapered. This is a short haircut in which the hair at the nape of the neck is cut very short and gradually gets longer and fuller at the crown area.

Bi-level. This is a drastic change in the lengths of hair from sides to back to bangs. Usually this is used with a drastically short haircut at the sides and a long, sometimes blunt cut at the back. Also lovingly known as *the mullet!*

Undercut. This can refer to two different looks. First, the hair is cut so that it will scoop under naturally or more easily when it is curled. The small amount right at the nape of the neck is cut to add appeal when the long hair is worn up off the neck.

ANDREA'S ADVICE

If you see someone with a haircut you like, ask her who her stylist is. Also, if your hair looks better when your stylist does it than when you do, ask him or her to teach you how to style your hair. Don't be shy—it's *your* hair. Plus, I usually consider the condition and style of the stylist's hair before I let him or her take a whack at mine! This may be just my own quirk, but I want my stylists to care about their own personal appearance as much as they care about mine.

Asymmetrical. The hair is not cut even on both sides. One side is cut shorter than the other side. This is generally done at a 45 degree angle but can be more severe for a more dramatic look.

Thinning. This means carefully cutting out small sections of extremely thick hair to make it appear thinner. Thinning is also used to "texture" the hair to give it a more lacy appearance.

Hairstyles often become fads. Asymmetrical cuts, spiked hair, and whatever drastic styles emerge on the scene are fad-type haircuts. Extremes in style are more difficult to change. Be stylish instead of faddish.

Simple Styles—Super Looks

There are countless numbers of styles for every hair type, texture, and length. Experimenting with styles lets you be creative. Add decorative clips, barrettes, combs, ribbons, scarves, bandannas, and bobby pins; even flowers and baby's breath added to your hair for special occasions give it a special look. These accessories are not only attractive, but they are also a great cure for hairdo blahs!

These styling terms will help you get the look you want, so know what they mean!

Q: "How can I add volume to my hair without making it super curly?"

A: Blow out your hair using a large round brush. Then take a section of hair starting at the crown, comb it straight up, lightly spritz it with hair spray, then wind it downward on an oversized Velcro roller. Spritz again. Repeat in areas where you want volume. Then, using your blow dryer on low, apply heat to each roller to make it form to the shape of the roller. Leave rollers in for 20 minutes or until completely cooled.

Styling Terms

Highlights—lifting or lightening color

Lowlights—adding deeper tones to create depth

Backcomb or tease—combing sections of hair backward (down) to the root, then smoothing the hair over the teased area; gives lift, volume, and control to your hair right where you want it

Bend—using heated styling tools to turn the ends under

Flip—using heated styling tools to turn the ends up

Movement—using anything that adds a sense of direction

Swoop—pulling long bangs across the forehead in a side-swept style; barely grazes the tips right above your brows

Volume—adding thickness

Lift—adding height

Upsweep—giving hair an upward direction (great for accenting your cheekbones)

What about styling aids such as mousses, setting gels, or lotions? These products help give holding power and direction to your hair. Follow the instructions on the package carefully. Always choose high-quality hair aids. Many of them, including hair spray, are high in alcohol, so use a water-soluble hair spray. Use products your stylist recommends. High-quality products mean high-quality hair. Check out some quality products at www.paulmitchell.com or www.matrix.com.

ANDREA'S ADVICE

Don't change your hairstyle based on your feelings or emotions on one particular day. When having a crummy or down day, we might decide that a drastic change in our appearance will lift our spirits and make us feel fresh and new. Yikes! When the excitement wears off, we can be left with an unwanted look or hair color. Subtle changes in style are easier to handle. Take time to think it through before you make style-changing and color-changing decisions.

Stylin' 'Dos

The sporty sass. Curl your hair all over your head, using a curling iron or hot rollers. When the curlers have cooled, remove them and run your fingers through your hair to separate the curls, therefore creating more curls. Lightly tease at the root to add desired lift—use pomade for chunky separations. If desired, pull one or both sides of your hair up loosely. Secure hair, using a decorative hair comb or barrette or bobby pins (place curls over the bobby pins to hide them). Apply a mist of hair spray.

The classic updo. Comb all of your hair back and off to one side. Secure with bobby pins up the center of your scalp if needed. Twist the rest of your hair toward the center of your head, creating a roll. Tuck the ends of your hair in the twist or twist them into a chignon (bun). Secure with hairpins or a decorative comb.

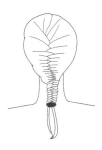

The fishtail braid. Comb your hair straight back, then pick up two sections of hair at the top of your head. Cross them right over left. Take a small amount of hair from the left side, above your ear, and add it to the section of hair you are holding on the right side. Repeat on the opposite side. Cross the two sections of hair again. Repeat these two steps until you reach the nape of your neck. You may stop here and make a ponytail or chignon, or add a bow. To continue the braid, take a small amount of hair from underneath one section, bring it around and over, and add it to the opposite section. When you reach the end of your hair, secure and tug on the braid to even out the tension.

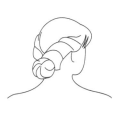

The roll-up. Brush one side of your hair up gently, then twist and tuck it into a roll. Hold it there with a barrette while you roll the other side. Pull the remaining hair together and twist it into a tight chignon. Bobby pin into place. Use hairpins or bobby pins to secure the two rolls. Cover the pins with a pretty bow.

The messy bun. Begin as if you are going to make a pony-tail (the placement doesn't matter—make it high or low). Wrap an elastic band around the ponytail until you have one more wrap to go, then pull your ponytail only three-quarters of the way through, leaving about two inches of the ends of your hair wrapped in the elastic band. Pull out pieces of the ponytail, making some long, some short—messy, messy, messy! Optional: Pull out a strand of hair by your bangs and wrap it behind your ear.

The fake-out. Looking for some length or curl or poof? The cleverly designed extensions or ready-to-wear hairpieces can make thin hair look thick or make shorter hair appear long. Today's extensions actually glue onto your natural hair at the root. This needs to be done by a pro. Try the clip-on extensions. These are a cinch to attach. Pull you hair back into a ponytail, but the last time through the rubber band, only pull the ponytail halfway out. Then attach the hairpiece around your ponytail. Work the fake curls into place to blend with your natural hair. Bobby pin the hairpiece to make it more secure. Choose a shade closest to your natural color.

The tousled tresses. Achieve this look by applying weightless pomade, then use your fingers to shake through your freshly styled hair. The disconnected look!

The curl girl. So you don't think you're good at making waves? No worries, I've got you covered. Try any of these methods to be a curl girl.

Large hot rollers. After hair is dry, roll three hot rollers on top and roll the rest vertically around your head. Remove rollers in five to eight minutes, finger comb, and spritz hair with freeze spray.

Macro Velcro rollers. Roll slightly damp hair, then blow dry right on these vented rollers. Remove rollers. These can also be used on dry hair to get a looser curl.

Pin curls. Grab a big handful of bobby pins (go for the large ones if you have thick hair), then twist two-inch sections of hair around your index finger. Secure the curl with a bobby pin. Typically, the longer you leave the pins in (like overnight), the better the curl.

Glam Tip: Wet hair? Unless it's corkscrew curly, blow it dry! Using a vented brush, pick up sections of your hair, directing the warm air toward the brush's bristles, and brush as you blow! This method allows you to control how your hair dries and gives it lift. Finish your hair off with a round, ceramic brush to smooth it. When hair is allowed to air dry it often looks heavy, oily, and dull. Want more tips on styling tools? Go to www.conair.com.

Glam Tip: If a piece of flyaway or stubborn hair refuses to stay where you put it, spray a cotton ball with hair spray and dab it directly on the stubborn spot.

It's All about Bangs

Bangs are a simple way to update your 'do. With bangs, it's practically anything goes! Here are some different styles you might consider:

Straight across. Chopping your bangs straight across is the classic look. It goes great with the traditional bob (all one length, no layers). Choose a long bang or short bang to make this pop.

Arched. The bangs are rounded evenly on both sides with the center being the shortest spot.

Thick or thin. If you have thick, full hair, you can keep your bangs the same, especially since that look is very in. It can give a heavy look to the bang, however. Or you can get the bangs thinned, allowing some of the forehead to be seen, which gives a lighter look.

Angled. Hair is parted to one side (permanently—you really can't switch sides with this bang), then angled beginning closest to the part. The severity of the angle will depend on how much funk you want!

Micro. These mini-bangs look great with an ultra-close cut or modern-day pixie (one inch all the way around). Blow dry while combing hair upward to give a more feminine twist to the spiked look. A touch of gel will keep it in place.

Coloring: Adding a Hue or Two

When it comes to color, take baby steps. In other words, start small. Begin by using a concentrated color mousse that washes out in eight to ten shampoos. It's easy to use and allows you to see what shade you might want to apply to your hair, should you choose to move up to a semi-permanent hair color. I personally like Color Pulse by L'Oréal Paris (www.loreal .com). This nonpermanent color in a nondrip mousse can even add shine and softness to your hair. It contains no ammonia or peroxide, which can be damaging. Follow the directions on the package, being sure to do the allergy test forty-eight hours prior to application. Always wear the gloves provided in the kit.

Coloring Tips

The first time you use a concentrated color mousse, don't leave it on as long as rec-

ANDREA'S ADVICE

Have you tried a truckload of styling products and tools, but your hair just won't do what you want it to? Let it do its own thing, its natural thing. Fighting your natural (God-given) hair bent steals lots of time. Part of loving yourself the way God designed you and seeing that you are beautiful in his eyes is accepting your hair. That's not to say you can't toss on a ball cap or stocking cap when it's acting totally wacky, but stressing about it, thinking the entire school is staring at it, or staying home because of it is just not okay! Don't give it that kind of power (same goes for a zit). Maybe—just maybe—someday you will see your hair as a blessing!

ommended unless your natural hair color is dark. Dark hair will not show as much of a contrast but will give highlights. Remember the longer you leave it on, the greater the color change.

Do not use this nonpermanent color on bleached or lightened hair as those strands will absorb more color, giving you a look you weren't expecting!

Do not color eyebrows or eyelashes at home. Go to a pro.

Get more tips at www.garnierusa.com.

Glam Tip: Want a new hair hue? Use caution! The least damaging color products are onetime-use colored mousses or comb-in temporary colors, followed by wash-in products that fade out. More serious categories include semi-permanent colors. These do not chemically change the hair shaft, so they are less damaging to your terrific tresses than permanent hair colors, which are the hardest on your hair! I suggest you have your trusted hairstylist apply the semi-permanent and permanent hair colors. They will use quality brands that may contain moisturizers to condition the hair and get it off to a good start.

Q: "I'm starting to get spring fever and want to highlight my hair! However, I don't want to go broke doing it. Can I possibly put in my own highlights?"

A: Most do-it-yourself kits are reasonably priced. But before you set up a home salon and go it alone, educate yourself by choosing a kit that is designed for simplicity and includes a highlighting tool! *Highlighting how-tos:* Start subtle on your first highlighting experience. You don't know yet if your hair absorbs color easily. Do the allergy test two days in advance and check your scalp for cuts or scrapes. Choose a color that is just a few shades lighter than your natural hair color. Nothing drastic. You can always go lighter next time. Always leave space between treated hair strands to avoid a run-together or patchy look.

Open the kit and take out the directions, the colorant, the developing crème, the protective gloves, the follow-up conditioner, and the tool. Lay everything out in front of you on an old towel. Read all

Things That Make Your Hair Go "Uck"

Okay, your hair doesn't have feelings, but these are the things it's not crazy about. Some you can control, some you just can't!

The wrong shampoo. Match products to your hair type and needs.

Too much conditioner. This creates major limp locks.

Alcohol-based styling products. These are way too drying for glam girl hair.

Bad perms. Go to a pro.

Poor eating habits. Healthy foods produce healthy hair.

Hormonal changes. Body chemistry can cause dryness, oiliness, less curl, tighter curl, or total limpness.

Environment. The humidity and air pollutants all matter.

Cigarette smoke. Cough, cough.

Medication. Certain drugs cause unexpected changes.

Stress. Knots in your stomach can cause hair loss and the release of certain chemicals that make hair tough to style.

You can see how your hair, even though it has no feeling, can be directly affected by what goes on *in* your body and what goes *into* your body.

directions and warnings. Decide where you want your highlights and what look you're going for: even or freestyle spacing, fine or chunky strands. Style and comb your dry and nonshampooed hair the way you usually wear it. Remember that if you style your hair differently, it will change the placement of the highlights. For instance, if you highlight while parted in the middle and then comb your hair to the right or left, the highlights might end up all on one side! Perhaps you will want to highlight the top and underneath. If you mess up, add some lowlights using a second kit, or give in and call your stylist!

Put on the official colorist gloves (feeling like a scientist, aren't you?) and prepare the mixture as directed. Immediately squirt a small amount of mixture on the highlighting tool, then beginning at the root (right at your scalp), slide the tool down the strand to the very tips. Reapply where needed to be sure the entire hair strand is saturated with the mixture. When finished, toss away the unused mixture.

Leave the mixture on according to the directions—but pay attention! Set a timer!

When time is up, very thoroughly rinse your hair using warm water—do not wash it. Apply conditioner, then rinse again.

Style away! You are officially highlighted!

Happy Thoughts on Bad Hair Days

"Are not five sparrows sold for two cents? Yet not one of them is forgotten before God. Indeed, the very hairs of your head are all numbered. Do not fear; you are more valuable than many sparrows" (Luke 12:6–7 NASB).

God knows the number and location of every strand on your beautiful head of hair. He knows the ones that get tangled in your brush, get blown away in the wind, and head down the drain. So what's the point? God is aware of and cares about every detail in your life—even your hair! In other words, you matter! Key word: **you!**

That is a fact worth turning over in your mind a time or two. Nothing about you goes unnoticed by your heavenly Father. Not your achievement awards, your joys, your hurt feelings, your physical aches, your flunked tests, your jammed locker, the friend who dissed you—nothing, nada, goes unnoticed.

On the days when life seems to bottom out, fix your mind on the fact that your heavenly Father is watching and is weaving the details of your life into a beautiful work of art. That, my young friend, will lead to happy days . . . no matter what your hair looks like!*

And we know that God causes everything to work together for the good of those who love God and are called according to his purpose for them.

Romans 8:28 NLT

*Get more encouraging tips for crummy days from my book *Happy Thoughts for Bad Hair Days.*

5

FaBULOUS NaiLS and Fancy FeeT

Hands are constantly on the move. Writing, scratching, playing sports, washing the dinner dishes (B.A.B.E.s *do* help around the house, right?)—the list goes on. And of course, everywhere our hands go, so do our nails.

Nails let us know when we have been ignoring them. They break, split, and chip. We get hangnails from dried-out cuticles. Well-cared-for nails can make our hands and fingers look longer and more graceful. Short, stubby nails may be a sign of a nail biter or nail picker, unless, of course, you keep your nails short for some practical reason such as sports, piano playing, or typing. I play the guitar, so the nails on my left hand are usually a little shorter than the ones on my right.

A weekly manicure helps keep your nails looking healthy. Even stubborn, hard-to-grow nails or weak, thin nails will benefit. If you feel embarrassed about your nails, a good manicure will help lift your spirits. You don't have to spend a ton of time, but do allow a minimum of thirty minutes for the whole process. Play your favorite CD and make your manicure an experience you enjoy.

Your Home Salon

Create your own home salon. Gather up cotton balls, Q-tips, a bowl of warm and soapy water, a nailbrush, enamel remover, a nonmetal file or emery board, nail clippers, a slant-tipped cuticle stick, cuticle remover cream, cuticle nippers, a nail buffer and buffing cream (for weak, thin nails), basecoat or clear nail hardener, enamel (polish), topcoat, nail oil, and hand lotion. If you have a ripped nail, have a repair kit handy too. Lay all the items out on a hand towel to protect the tabletop from enamel and remover.

Sounds as if you need a suitcase to gather it all up, but you won't! Store your nail products in a large, clear Ziploc bag, a cosmetic bag, or a small basket. That way they're all together when you need them.

Manicure Magic

Going through a complete, detailed manicure step-by-step is the best method for learning how to care for your nails. Though this may seem complicated, once you catch on it will be a cinch! Having a salon manicure to watch how it's done is also helpful—but don't get hooked.

Starting Clean

Wet a 100 percent cotton ball or pad with nail polish remover. Press it gently on your nails for five seconds, then wipe off all old polish. Try using a remover-dipped Q-tip to reach remaining polish along the edges of the nail.

Take a quick inventory of your nails. Are some longer than others? Are your cuticles dry and cracked? Any hangnails or ridges? How about splitting or weak nails? Any clipped polish? If you answered *yes* to any of these questions, you've been ignoring your nails!

Filing Down and Shaping Up

Choose your shape—oval or square. Using a medium-grained file (150–180) or the rough side of an emery board, file from the side of your nail toward the center. Let the outer corner grow straight up a fraction of an inch, then angle toward the center. This method makes your nails stronger and less prone to ripping. Never saw back and forth! File in one direction or you'll force the nail dust down between the nail layers, possibly causing them to split.

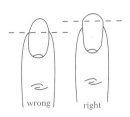

Never cut your nails with scissors. Use clippers if you need to shorten, even out, or preshape your nail. When your nails are a nice shape, finish off the edges with the fine (200–400) side of the emery board.

To determine the length of your nails, answer these questions:

What are my daily activities? _____

_____

How fast do my nails grow? _____

_____

What's my favorite look? _____

_____

Perhaps keeping your nails short for sports is practical. Super-long nails are more prone to breaking (and look like claws if they get out of hand). Medium-length nails are typically stronger and easier to work with. Rarely do my nails grow longer than one-eighth inch over the *ends* of my fingers. Until my thirteenth birthday, I picked and bit my nails. Then my dad gave me a sapphire ring (my birthstone) with a small diamond on each side. When I slid the ring on my finger I thought, *This pretty ring just can't be on a hand with chewed-up nails.*

Do you bite your nails? If it's hard for you to stop, try brushing on one of those awful-tasting nail biters' products. It will help you have self-control—and nice nails!

Soften with Suds

Soak the ends of your fingers in warm, soapy water for two minutes to loosen and soften the cuticle (the rim of skin that surrounds the nail). Why not take a few deep breaths and chill while you wait? Rinse and pat dry.

Cuticle Care

Apply cuticle remover cream (or hand lotion) to each cuticle and gently massage it in. It doesn't actually remove the cuticle; it prepares the cuticle to be pushed back so it doesn't grow up while attached to the nail—this *will* cause the cuticle to split. Yuck. Use the slanted edge of a cuticle stick to gently push the cuticle back toward the knuckle. Never cut your cuticle off. It is there to protect the nail base from infection. Always keep your cuticles well moisturized with hand lotion or night cream.

Scrub and Rub

Scrub your nails with a soft-bristle nailbrush or toothbrush dipped in warm, soapy water. Rinse and pat dry.

Clipping Corners

Clip away any hangnails using cuticle nippers. Be sure you don't clip too closely and cut the skin.

ANDREA'S ADVICE

If dry, cracking cuticles are an ongoing problem for you, try soaking your nails in warm olive oil before bedtime. Pat off the excess—don't wash it off.

Buffing Up Some Beauty

If your nails bend, peel, or split, give them a buffing session twice a week. This helps them grow and gives them added strength and a smoother surface (good-bye ridges). The buffing action stimulates blood circulation, which nourishes and encourages growth. It also allows the protein, collagen, or vitamins in the buffing cream to penetrate the nail.

Apply a good buffing cream to your entire nail. Using a deerskin or other high-quality buffer, buff across your nail in one direction, using the full length of the buffer. Continue until buffing cream is gone and a natural shine develops. Rescrub your nail to remove buffing residue. Keep your buffer clean by wiping it with a clean towel after each use. Buffing takes time, but it is the best treatment for weak, thin, slow-growing nails.

Glam Tip: Make a habit of munching on a few raw carrots every day to get the vitamin A you need for stronger nails. It's great for your skin and hair too.

A Strong Base

Once your nails are dry, brush on basecoat to seal them. You can stop here if colored enamel is not for you. Some girls might think it's reserved for frilly girls. But manicures are for everyone! The shiny, clear look is very appropriate for daytime wear or for busy schedules. Basecoat applied before enamel will keep your nails from turning yellow from the enamel itself. For weak, thin nails, use clear nail hardener or strengthener instead of basecoat.

Glam Tip: A good inner-nail strengthener is gelatin, but you need to take it daily for several months before you see any results. Gelatin comes in capsules or powder that can be added to fruit juice. Check out Knox for Nails in the Jell-O aisle!

Painting Pretty

To paint or not to paint? That is the question! If you decide to splash on some color, apply one or two thin coats of professional-formula enamel. Look for brands that are formaldehyde and toluene free by reading the bottle. These ingredients, though they make the enamel dry faster, are harmful to your body. Enamel is also available in strengthening, chip resistant, and long lasting. Choose the one that fits your needs. Allow the first coat fifteen minutes to dry completely before you add the second coat. This prevents smudges and dent marks. To polish, use the three-stroke method—once down each side of the nail, then once down the center. Be sure you coat the edge of your nail tip to help prevent chipping.

To create a more together look and to keep harmony in your overall color scheme, select enamel in the same color family as your blush and lip gloss (either warm or cool). Light colors are appealing and graceful looking. They also make chips less noticeable (which is why I usually wear white frost). Dark polishes make the nails look heavy and smaller. Decorative polishing such as stripes, polka dots, flowers, glitter, or decals are fun, but they can be too trendy, so use them sparingly. Enamel is supposed to enhance your nails—not scream for attention!

Glam Tip: Make sure to keep the cap tightly closed between applications. When enamel becomes thick, add a few drops of thinner or buy a new bottle. Want to keep your favorite nail polishes from becoming gooey, hard, or oldy-moldy? Store them in the fridge! Just remove the bottle fifteen to thirty minutes before you want to apply it so it will be back to room temp.

No Smudges

Remove any enamel you get on your skin or cuticle with a cotton tip dipped in polish remover. A handy remover-filled pen with a sponge tip applicator works well too.

Top It Off

Now you're ready to apply a clear topcoat or a clear nail hardener over the entire nail. Don't forget to brush some under the nail tip for added protection against chipping. If desired, now is the time to spray on a quick-drying product. Reapply the topcoat the day after your manicure for a longer-lasting effect.

The Finishing Touch

For the professional-looking finish with a well-moisturized touch, apply a small amount of nail oil on the cuticle area. Massage it in carefully. Take a look. Was it worth the time? Repeat your manicure weekly, adding or changing enamel when necessary. Perhaps the best time to manicure is when you can allow a total drying time of thirty to forty-five minutes. This can be after homework is done, while watching TV, or right before bed.

The French Flare

Have you always liked the look of the French manicure but can't afford to have it done at a nail salon? You're in luck. There are several do-it-yourself kits available in the nail-product sections of most grocery stores or drugstores. But you might already own some of what you need to achieve your desired look. If so, just fill in the rest! Here's how:

1. Shape your nails so they are square instead of rounded.
2. Apply one coat of clear basecoat. Dry five minutes.
3. Using the tip of the applicator brush sideways, apply a thin line of pure white enamel across the top of your nails. Dry five minutes.

ANDREA'S ADVICE

If you are going to wear nail polish, be responsible with it. As soon as it begins to chip off, reapply more polish or take it all off. Do not peel the polish off your nails! You can damage your nail by pulling off the top layer. Carry either remover pads or enamel in your purse to avoid the temptation to pick it off!

4. Apply a very pale pink polish over the entire nail—yes, even on the white tip. When it's totally dry, add a second coat of the pink!

There you are! A B.A.B.E. with a French manicure.

> **Glam Tip:** When your nail rips or tears near the edge, it's still possible to save it. But if the rip is deep or long you might as well face it—the nail will have to go! When you trim the broken nail, be sure to trim *all* of your nails a little. To leave a few long and a few short looks unkempt and jagged. For those you can save, purchase a nail-repair kit. Follow the enclosed directions carefully. Be sure the fiber paper you adhere to your nails is flat—no wrinkles, creases, or air bubbles! Tear the paper off the sheet rather than cutting it. This will blend in more naturally with the nail surface. Always apply enamel over repaired nails. These nail-repair methods never really heal the rip, but they prolong cutting the nail off until it has grown longer.

Q: "I really want my nails to look good the first week back at school, but they are short because I bite them—I know, I'm not supposed to do that. Even so, what can I do?"

A: Right—you should not bite your nails! So this info will help you with your bad habit and your length since you are nail challenged! Take a drive to your local drugstore or beauty supply store, head to the nail section, and snag a set of instant self-stick nails that will give you the well-cared for, long-nail look without the hassle of glue or expensive salon prices. Plus, they're impossible to bite, so your natural nail will get a chance to grow. To apply, follow the directions on the package.

Get Pressed Into It

Whether they are glue-on or self-stick, press-on nails can spice up your nails in an instant. Though they are great for that one-time special occasion, make them temporary. Your natural nails need to breathe to remain strong and healthy. Besides, we've all seen some artificial nails on teens that look really fake—like they're playing dress up. If you give the nails a try—whether it's to cover a torn nail that is growing out, to even up a nail that is too short, or to help you stop biting your nails—use them sparingly.

Prepolished glue-on and self-stick nails have a reputation for popping off at the most inconvenient times. They've been reported to have shown up in soup bowls, clogged drains, or another person's ponytail! So follow directions carefully for do-it-yourself nails. Hint: If the directions say to press and hold for thirty seconds, do it! Be sure to file nails to a reasonable length. If you want to change the color, change the nail!

Glam Tip: Line up the end of the press-on nail with the center of your cuticle, then gently lower it onto your nail. Once in place, press and hold for ten seconds. If any nail has a rough edge, just file it away. Always remove the nails after three or four days or as soon as you see them lifting around the edges to prevent bacteria from being lodged under the nail. Dispose of nails—don't save them to reuse.

Eight Hand and Nail Nuggets

1. Wear rubber gloves when you need to have your hands in water for a prolonged period of time (like when you wash dishes, mop the floor, give the cat a bath, or hand wash your delicates). Nails soften in warm water—not to mention the wrinkling effect on your fingertips.
2. Nails become brittle in cold weather, so wear gloves or mittens to keep them warm in those winter months. (The fingerless gloves don't do it!)
3. Don't worry about any white spots under your nails. They are usually air pockets that form as your nail grows. Never fear—they eventually grow right out the top of your nail.
4. Keep an emergency nail kit in your locker, backpack, or purse.
5. Don't use your nails as tools to open envelopes and boxes, untie knots, remove staples, or pick trapped food from your teeth.
6. Nails freshly polished? Pick up things with the pads of your fingers.
7. Keep hand cream near the kitchen and bathroom sinks to use after you wash

Find more great info on nails and such at www.nailene.com or www.sallyhansen.com.

your hands. Carry a tube of hand cream in your purse or backpack for on-the-spot use.

8. Use a rich, heavy cream or petroleum jelly on your hands at night, and wear white cotton gloves while you sleep. Cotton gloves are also good protectors while you do housework or outdoor work. If anyone teases you about wearing gloves, tell him or her you're just giving the house the white-glove test!

Helping Hands

Hands are our instruments of love. We greet, hug, and help each other with our hands. The Bible indicates we are God's hands and feet here on earth. That means we are used by God to reach out to others, expressing the Lord's love through our actions and touch. He uses us in loving ways for his eternally significant purposes.

Proverbs 31:20 teaches us that the woman who fears (honors and respects) God—young or old—is to extend her hands to the poor and stretch out her hands to the needy. This woman cares what happens in the lives of others. You are this (young) woman!

Jesus's hands healed, loved, comforted, and—most of all—were scarred for us. Jesus's nail-scarred hands provide forgiveness of sins, health, and eternal life for us today—right now. Open yourself up to being his instrument of love. Let your hands be used like his.

ANDREA'S ADVICE

Acrylic or gel nails are great come prom night if your natural nails are looking shabby. But they get very expensive and require time-consuming trips to a manicurist. Yeah, I know that's fun, but for the day-to-day stuff, go natural. Learn to care for your own nails—you're going to have them forever! Don't expect your parents to fork out the cash (even if other parents do) for something you *can* do on your own.

Glam Tip: For the ultimate in hand and feet pampering, treat yourself to heated beauty mittens and booties. Check them out at www.discount beautycenter.com. Ooh la la!

Q: "I am embarrassed to say that I have corns on my feet. How can I get rid of them?"

A: No need to be embarrassed. Corns are often the natural result of friction from wearing shoes that rub excessively against the skin of your precious feet. Try to figure out which footwear is rubbing you wrong, then get them stretched, or always be sure you wear thick socks with those shoes.

Now about those corns. First, pamper the area with a sudsy foot soak in warm water. This will soften the built-up, calloused tissue. Then apply corn remover pads. These handy little guys provide a protective cushion for the corn while delivering some beta hydroxy right to the corn. Once the corn disappears, apply a heavy foot cream on a regular basis to keep skin smooth and soft.

Q: "My heels are so dried out and crackly looking. Any suggestions?"

A: Get rid of the dry, dead skin and moisturize at the same time right out of your own kitchen cupboards. This all-natural recipe calls for only two ingredients: cornmeal and avocado oil or olive oil. The cornmeal will exfoliate and the oil will moisturize.

Cornmeal moisturizing scrub. In a small bowl, blend together $\frac{1}{4}$ cup cornmeal (not cornstarch) with 1 tablespoon avocado or olive oil. Keeping your heels over the tub, gently rub the mixture on your heels in a circular motion. Pay special attention to all calloused areas. Rinse with warm, soapy water. Apply your favorite moisturizer. Then treat your hands with the leftover mixture. Sweet!

ANDREA'S ADVICE

Take special care of your feet! They're the instrument used to walk your babe-a-licious self into the lives of others, telling them about the God you serve and the Jesus you love. See for yourself. "How beautiful are the feet of those who bring good news!" (Romans 10:15 NIV). Good news! That's the gospel message. Do you have beautiful feet?

Fancy Feet

Even your feet, toes, and toenails need an occasional beauty treatment to keep them fun, fresh, and fancy looking. *Pedicure* is the technical name for a nail treatment on your toenails.

Follow the same steps on your toenails we outlined for fingernails, making adjustments where needed. Soak your feet in warm water in a basin or bathtub. Instead of filing your toenails to an oval shape, simply cut them straight across. Then file to smooth out any rough edges. No need to ruin a pair of perfectly good nylons with rough toenails.

Apply enamel year-round. I know if the snow falls you're not going to be wearing sandals, so no one will see your ten toes. Not true! You will see them every day. If you love the look and feel of painted toes, go for it.

Feet have a tendency to get dry, chapped, calloused, and rough. Soak or cream your feet regularly to avoid these conditions. A pumice, loofah pad, or sloughing cream are all wonder-workers for removing dry, dead skin.

A little special attention, and your feet will feel refreshed—and they'll step a little higher!

6

STYLIN'

Remote in hand as I scanned through the channels, I found myself in amazement. Whoever imagined there'd be entire networks broadcasting shopping channels or fashion channels or decorating channels! Sitting in the comfort of our jammies and cozied up on the couch, we can bring jewelry, handbags, makeup, shoes, and hair tools right into our homes—literally any time of the day or night. Thankfully, I'm not personally into shopping like that (I know people who are hooked and sit for hours every day viewing stuff that they really don't need and can't afford), but I will confess this: I've fallen for the style channel. Yeah, I'm into the clothing thing. Not buying them, but watching how fabrics, colors, shapes, belts, hats—you name it—are used to achieve certain looks. You can create endless looks (though there are eight basic clothing personalities I'll inform you of). Plus, have you experienced the sheer joy of watching the show's host take an expensive designer outfit, then hit the mall to recreate the same look for less than a hundred bucks? That's being a smart and savvy shopper. I've been teaching some of these techniques for years and love picking up new tips off the tube. Besides, the current host is so adorable to watch. She gets *almost* as excited as I do! And I've made up my own game. Want to know what it is? Keep reading.

God, Then Gap

Oftentimes we are shown hot looks that flash hot bods (you know what I mean). Some of the outfits are cool but not quite right. Being who I am and given what I believe as a B.A.B.E., my brain automatically analyzes the stylin'-but-skimpy looks and figures out how to transform them into totally modest looks. Modest? Yep. We may as well talk about it right up front!

I define modesty as dressing in ways that honor God. The stores are chock-full of revealing, body-clinging styles that are all about showing skin and shape. In our sex-saturated society, wearing this stuff sends certain messages. Unfortunately, our world cares less about the clothes that cover and more about revealing the bod that's underneath them. So as God's girls who are called to be set apart, to be different, to not do everything the way the narcissistic (pleasing only yourself) world around us does, our aim is to make it modest. That doesn't mean we can't follow styles; it just means sometimes we'll have to be a little more creative with them. How exciting to make it a personal challenge, a game—just to see what cool looks you can come up with! That's what I do, and it makes watching those shows and strolling the mall even more fun. So it's like this: put God first, then the styles you see on TV or at Gap, Wet Seal, Limited, or wherever. I hope you'll join me in my little game playing.

Here's my other huge challenge: to tell you everything I can about fashion, shopping, styles, color, line, fabrics, caring for your clothes, and organizing your wardrobe—*all* in this one chapter. Impossible. So here's the deal. The info I

Layer, layer, layer! It's the easiest way to take an "iffy" outfit and make it wearable as a B.A.B.E.! Tuck long tanks or A-shirts into low-rise jeans to avoid the dreaded "crack attack" and hide your precious stomach skin. Double up shirts to create a higher neckline and cover cleavage. In other words, keep your secret places secret!

really want to say to you is here. The other stuff is on my website, www.andreastephens.com, under Hot Topics: Stylin'. I'll also toss you some other cool fashion-related sites to check out.

That said, let's jump in.

Your Clothing Personality

You have a personality. That's no news flash. But did you know you have a clothing personality? It's true. Pay attention to what kinds of things you're drawn to, and you'll probably notice a pattern. Though clothing likes and dislikes can change from high school to college and so on, you will fit into one or two of these personality styles. Why does this matter? Because it will save you time (you'll know what style you're shopping for) and money (you'll make fewer crazy purchases), and you'll know yourself a little better. Like it or not, fair or not, clothes talk. They spill the dish, giving insights into our inner world, our attitudes, and the like.

You want to look at different fashion styles and eventually create a wardrobe that fits your personality and works together, helping you get the most out of every piece of clothing hanging in your closet. Having a wardrobe that works—that's functioning fashion!

Read the definitions to get the dish on your personal style.

The classic personality. You feel your best in tailored (slightly fitted), timeless styles. It's the clothes that stay in style year after year that are you!

The dramatic personality. You go for the exotic fashion extremes that the average person would not dare to wear—the stuff that struts down designer runways.

The sporty-natural personality. Casual clothes with an athletic touch are for you. The same is true of the fabrics you like—forget the shiny, fancy stuff. You're a no-nonsense dresser.

The romantic personality. Your favorite styles are frilly and feminine. Ruffles, soft lace, flowing designs and fabrics—you love 'em.

The ingénue personality. The baby doll, girlish look is what you like best. It's the puffy stuff!

The flash-fad personality. You love what pops up on the fashion scene and want to be the first to wear it. But it's history the second something new appears popular.

The contemporary personality. You prefer the fashionable look of toned-down fads. Nothing extreme, nothing old-fashioned. You like the trends but don't overdo it.

Which personality just screams **you**? _____

Savvy Shopping for Fashionistas

Shopping. You love to do it, you sorta have to do it, so learn how to do it the best way! Don't be a sloppy shopper, be a savvy shopper! A savvy shopper thinks before she acts. Here are some super tips to help you make better clothing decisions and help you spend less time standing at the closet wondering what in the world to wear!

Take inventory. First, take out of your closet anything that's worn, stained, or in need of repair. Second, weed out the stuff that doesn't fit anymore. Third, say good-bye to anything you have not worn in over a year (okay, if it has sentimental value, you can keep it a little longer). Now, make a list of what basics you are missing, like a black skirt, a pair of khakis, a white or ivory blouse, and so on. Add to the list the things you need to buy in order to turn single items into outfits. For instance, if you have two multicolored shirts, both with a touch of plum, then purchasing a plum skirt gives you two new outfits. Get it?

Look, then leap. Look around before you lay down your money! If

Mags, department stores, and TV shows can give us cool dressing ideas, but we don't have to arrange our outfits just like store mannequins or movie stars. Pick and choose what fits your personality and what you're comfortable wearing. It's more important to wear what looks *good* on you than to wear the latest style.

possible, make your shopping adventure a two-part process. On the first trip to the stores, get a preview of what's out there. Check styles, colors, fabrics, themes, and prices. Think about which pieces will freshen up your wardrobe and give you a look that's *you*, all for the best price. (Speaking of price, don't bust your budget on clothes—it's not worth it.) Now you're ready for your second trip to shop, shop, shop!

Buy complete outfits. In addition to filling in the gaps of your current wardrobe by getting pieces that complete an outfit, buy complete outfits. This is one of the biggest mistakes teens make. They buy a shirt here, get some pants there. That's almost like being an impulse shopper—buying with very little thought! Purchasing complete outfits will save you the grief of standing in your closet trying to match stuff together.

Explore departments. Are you stuck in one department or do you cross-shop? I'm sure your fingers comb their way through the juniors department first—that's natural. However, the juniors department is the trendiest department. Expand into the misses once in a while.

Be a copycat shopper. You should study the popular brands and the designer lines so you can find look-alikes for half the cost. With many lines, you pay extra money for the name on the label. Forget that! Go for well-made items at moderate prices.

Shop for quality, not quantity. Your shopping goal should not be simply to load your closet with clothes. With lower-quality clothes you may be able to stretch your dollar, but chances are the clothes won't hold up. Do a quality check on the buttons, zipper, seams, and top stitching.

Check your mood. In a wild and crazy mood? That might cause you to buy something you'll never be brave enough to wear in public. The opposite can be true too. If you're feeling blue, you might go for the frumpy, baggy clothes in dark colors that you won't even *want* to wear once you snap out of your murky mood. So know how you feel, and buy when you feel like *you*!

Beauty Bonus with BarlowGirl: "Romans 12:2 tells us not to conform. So no matter how loud the world screams with their styles, we believe God is bigger than that. We don't need to blend or just be average," Alyssa shares. Lauren explains, "We are all about layers when it comes to style." Rebecca adds, "We always try to add a feminine touch—like the chains hanging off my belt are mixed with rhinestones and pearls. Lauren has a studded belt that's pink."

Know a timeless classic from a flashy fad. Classic styles don't go in and out of fashion. For instance, five-pocket jeans, turtlenecks, blazers, and straight-cut skirts are always in style. Classics make the best investments. Fads are those unique or funky styles that are hot for a short time, but once that time is over, you wouldn't want to be caught in them. To avoid wasting money on fads, simply purchase one or two fads each season, just enough to keep you looking stylish. But keep this in mind: just because a look is popular doesn't mean you should wear it. Skip the low-cut tops, mini-mini skirts, hipster denims, or lacey, sheer fabrics. Choose to dress your body like a princess B.A.B.E.; after all, you are the daughter of the King.

Accessorize yourself. Very often a basic style can get that up-to-the-minute look by adding the coolest accessory—belt, bag, shoes, jewelry. Here's where you can have fun and express yourself! I personally love bling! Bling (I call it glitz) is always in: glass beads, crystal, rhinestones, sequins. In the past, sparkle was kept for eveningwear or special occasions only. Today it's splashed into everyday outfits. Try it. If it feels as if you're playing dress up, it's not for you.

Plan ahead with prints and polka dots. If you like clothes with flower prints or bold stripes or tra-

Q: "My parents are not keen on the idea of me getting my ears pierced. I'm fourteen and it makes me feel like a baby. What should I do?"

A: I'm glad you've not gone behind your parents' backs and gotten your ears pierced without their permission. That would definitely not be the way to handle the situation. I suggest you talk to them again, asking if you may wear magnetic earrings. They look just like pierced. Styles are limited, but you'll get the basic look you want. Be conservative and you'll calm your parents' fears and gain their trust.

ditional plaids, that's great. Just keep in mind that you can't wear them all together! As a general rule (and especially for a limited budget), choose to buy solid bottoms (pants, skirts, shorts) and printed tops, or vice versa.

Be color conscious. Choose three to five colors that make you look and feel your best. When you purchase tops and bottoms in these hues (or in ones that coordinate with these hues), you will automatically expand your wardrobe. This gives you mix-n-match ability!

Know when enough is enough. Don't overbuy on the same item. You probably don't need seven pairs of jeans, especially when you're going to a dress-up event and have no slacks to wear! Create a well-rounded wardrobe so you will have the right outfit for every occasion, from school to church to a night out with friends to attending a wedding with your family!

Approach sale racks with caution. What appears to be a bargain may not be. Ask yourself, "Is this item on the sale rack because it's not made well, or because it's off-color, damaged, or soon to be out of style? Does this fabric require expensive dry cleaning?" Occasionally you really can get great deals, but always get tags and think twice before purchasing from the sale rack.

Shop with one or two trusted friends. Group shopping is perfect when you're just cruising the mall for fun. But it's too difficult to make savvy shopping decisions when they're all giving you their opinions (some will like it, some won't). On serious shopping sprees, go with one or two trusted friends or your parents. Oh, don't be intimidated by pushy salespeople either!

Being a savvy shopper is a real art, huh? It's worth it. Just like the woman described in Proverbs 31 who searches out and thinks out her purchases, you too will be considered virtuous when it comes to the whole clothing thing!

ANDREA'S ADVICE

Become familiar with brands and designers—there will be some who continuously design according to your clothing tastes. This makes shopping more practical because when you buy within the same few lines, you'll find outfits that coordinate in color and style, giving you a wardrobe that works together.

Balance Your Bod

What looks good on you? Which styles are best for dressing your figure? Do the fabrics you select really matter? Let's investigate.

Use of line. Lines created by stripes, seams, pleats, detailed designs, or even a row of buttons are tools in achieving your desired look. Horizontal lines add width. Vertical lines add an illusion of height and slenderness. Curved lines on collars, ruffles, or seams add fullness and softness. Diagonal lines add height and minimize size. All of these are illusions. You don't actually become taller or wider or slimmer. Nonetheless, using line creativity can help you dress to enhance your figure.

Use of style. The cut and style of a garment can affect your figure's appearance by affecting its proportion. Remember, there is no "ideal" figure like our culture tries to make us believe. God made us unique and individual, and there is no such thing as a "right" or "wrong" figure type. However, there is a sense of balance and proportion that you can achieve in your dressing. Use a garment's style to balance your features.

Here's a simple rule to follow: avoid repeating the size and shape of your features with the style and line of the clothing design. For instance, if you have broad shoulders or large breasts, wearing blouses, wraps, or shirts with pleats or lots of detail-

Do you feel like a fashion frump if you don't wear the newest styles? Well, stop it! Every style is not for you. Don't let fashion designers or magazines dictate your wardrobe. Be okay with not wearing *exactly* what others are wearing. This is great training in learning to be your own person and preparing to think for yourself on more important issues.
Is it true that a one-piece swimsuit could be more hip and slenderizing than a two-piece? Check it out at—you guessed it, my website!

ing on the upper part might make you look like a football player. Likewise, if you have hips that are wider than your shoulders, wearing a pleated bohemian-type skirt would emphasize your hips. None of this makes your shoulders, breasts, or hips wrong! And it's totally okay to chuck all fashion "guidelines" and wear what you want.

Use of fabrics. The fabric you choose can add to or take away from the look you're going for. As a general rule, heavier fabrics, nubby knits, and stiff textures add *visual* weight to your figure. So do shiny-surfaced fabrics because they reflect light. Smooth, soft-fitting fabrics with dull or matte finishes will not add the visual weight.

FYI: Cotton, wool, linen, and silk are natural fabrics (nature-made). Polyester, spandex, rayon, nylon, and velour are synthetics (man-made).

Glam Tip: Wear prints and plaids that are the same size scale as your figure. Petite figures that wear large prints look overwhelmed. So it goes for larger figures that choose tiny prints. Choose those that best fit your body size. This same principle applies to your accessories (jewelry, belts, scarves, and purses). Select accessories proportionate to your body size.

Q: "I got into a discussion with my friends about wearing spaghetti-strap tops in the heat of summer. We didn't all agree. What's your opinion?"

A: Let me toss out a few things for you and your friends to think about (then you can pray about what you should do). First, spaghetti-strap tops with exposed bra straps look messy. I'm not the fashion police, but it's just sorta tacky. I know tons of girls do it, so if that's you, choose either a bra with clear straps or a bra with the same color strap as your top.

Second, a spaghetti-strap top gives the impression that a girl is not *wearing* a bra since there's no evidence of a bra strap (the same is true of tube tops and halter tops).

ANDREA'S ADVICE

If you are living a life of God-worship, the result is that "you don't fuss about what's on the table at mealtimes or whether the clothes in your closet are in fashion. There is far more to your life than the food you put in your stomach, more to your outer appearance than the clothes you hang on your body" (Matthew 6:25 Message).

Some girls wear a strapless bra with spaghetti straps. Some clothing companies are making these tops with built-in bras. Both of these are good. But allow me to emphasize that the first glance gives the impression of bralessness. Couple that impression with bare shoulders, and a girl possibly creates an enticing combination for the guys (and men) who are looking.

Plus, there is absolutely no reason for a girl's nipples to be visible through her shirt! No one has the right to see the size or shape of your private areas. Keep your secret places secret. Wear a bra and make it a lightly padded one.

Third, check yourself. Take the sit and bend test. With spaghetti strap tops—or any top, for that matter—check to make sure your lower back is not showing when you sit down. Now bend forward. Can you see cleavage? If so, it's cut too low. Shorten the straps to bring it up a bit.

Last, ask your dad or brother what they think. If they are brave enough to be honest, their answer might settle the issue for you. These are a few things to chew on with your friends. Because people have differing views, you may never all agree, but I'm proud of you for talking about these issues!

"Let not yours be the [merely] external adorning with [elaborate] interweaving and knotting of the hair, the wearing of jewelry, or changes of clothes; but let it be the inward adorning and beauty of the hidden person of the heart, with the incorruptible and unfading charm of a gentle and peaceful spirit" (1 Peter 3:3–4 AMP).

Organizing Your Wardrobe—Seriously!

If you're like most other teens, your clothes are jammed into your closet, some hanging half off the hanger, some inside out, others buttoned wrong, and several in desperate need of an iron or laundry basket. I wouldn't doubt that many of you even have clothes on doorknobs, on bedposts, over chairs, or—the worst—on the floor! Well, not anymore! You'll be less stressed (and so will the laundry person in the house) when you are organized and able to see your wardrobe clearly! Let's get started.

First, unclutter your closet. Get out all the things you haven't worn in the last year. Allow your wardrobe some breathing space. Ask yourself why you haven't worn these garments—they don't fit, they're out of style, they need repairs, they're worn and tattered looking, or you just have nothing to go with them.

Take your pile of "don't wear" and drop it off at your church's clothing drive or your local thrift shop. I also try to stick to my personal fair-exchange policy. If I want a new dress, I give one away. If I need new slacks, I find someone who can wear the ones that don't fit me anymore. It makes it so much fun to give things away. Then I don't feel as if I've wasted those other purchases, and at the same time I'm weeding out the optional clothes, allowing myself a wardrobe that's more workable.

Make a pile of "repairs." A missing button can put your favorite blouse or dress out of order! If you can't find the original button, go buy a complete new set for the garment. Buttons, zippers, snaps, and thread for hems are not expensive! Fixing your repair pile will give you more to wear.

Separate your clothes. Separate clothes into the two major times of year: spring/summer and fall/winter. If you live in a warm climate year-round as I do, just keep your cool-weather clothes in the back of your closet for easy access on those chilly evenings. Put the clothes you're not presently wearing in a garment bag or cover them with a clean plastic bag (with the exception of leather, suede, and furs, as this damages them). When storing wools and sweaters, use mothballs in drawers and bags. Keep the mothballs or flakes from touching your garments.

When the seasons begin to change and you uncover your sleeping beauties, you'll feel as if you have a new wardrobe. The effect is not the same if you've been staring at the same clothes all year round.

Group your garments. Now you're ready to group your clothes according to type: blouses, shirts (including active-wear T-shirts and sweatshirts), jackets, jeans, pants, shorts, skirts, dresses, and sweaters. Arrange them from light shades to dark shades. I go one step farther with my blouses, separating short-sleeved from long-sleeved. Now you have a clear view of your wardrobe! Do you like what you see? Are you stressing less? Good! Give a sigh of relief and treat yourself to a bubble bath!

Glam Tip: Store earrings in empty egg cartons (remove the top portion). Put one pair per space. It's easy and inexpensive. To go a step fancier, get the clear acrylic padded jewelry trays that fit nicely on a shelf or inside a drawer. Some even have adjustable compartments to accommodate earring size. Plus, they're stackable. It you can't find them in a store, try www.stacksandstacks.com.

Glam Tip: Choose your necklace length and shape to complement the neckline of your garment. Necklaces crossing the neckline give a choppy look. For boat-neck and crewneck designs, wear a short, choker-type necklace. Note: Lots of today's necklaces, earrings, and bracelets are actually decorative designs and symbols that make statements you might not even be aware of! Six-sided crystals, zodiac signs, the yin-yang symbol, mood rings, eyeballs, bird feet with claws, skeletons, and snakes are linked to dark occult beliefs. They may seem harmless, but they're tied in with powerful practices. In refusing to wear these symbols, you give honor to the One *you* serve. If you're into symbols, wear the ones on "our side"! Crosses, angels, fish symbols, and True Love Waits rings all point to Christianity!

Q: "I got my ears pierced a couple months ago but find that most earrings bother my ears. What should I do?"

A: Choose earrings with nickel-free posts or wires. Nickel seems to irritate sensitive skin. You can also try sterling silver earrings, or the 14 karat or 24 karat gold posts, which work for almost everyone.

Dressed Like a Divine Diva

As a Christian and a B.A.B.E., you are divine! A bit of divinity himself, the Holy Spirit, lives inside of you (1 Corinthians 6:19–20). Plus, according to God's promises, we share in his divine nature (2 Peter 1:3–4). Divine, indeed.

And that diva part? You are beautiful in the eyes of the One who created you *on* purpose and *for* a purpose. You've got style, flare, and a look that is yours alone.

My point? Being a divine diva has everything to do with *you* on the inside, including the way you dress. The Bible talks about clothing or dressing from the inside out. Here's what to put on!

> Clothe yourselves with humility toward one another, for God is opposed to the proud, but gives grace to the humble.
>
> 1 Peter 5:5 NASB

We can choose to "put on" this attitude of humbleness. To be humble is to have a grateful appreciation of who God has created you to be: a servant, not to be served, having all of your actions and attitudes motivated by love.

> Put on a heart of compassion.
>
> Colossians 3:12 NASB

Compassion is having feelings of concern and love toward others, being able to see them and their struggles through eyes of understanding and love, then being moved to take action to help them.

Don't know what to do with a stain? Don't know if colored clothes are washed in hot or cold water? Don't know which hangers are okay for sweaters? Stop right now, rush to my website, and read "Proper Care for Long-Lasting Wear" under Hot Topics: Stylin'!

Put on the full armor of God . . . the breastplate of righteousness . . . the shield of faith . . . the helmet of salvation, and the sword of the Spirit, which is the word of God.

Ephesians 6:11, 14, 16, 17 NASB

Just as we dress ourselves for daily activities, so we can dress for spiritual activities. The armor of God is given to us as our spiritual outfit. Dress in it every single day! Then you will be ready for any occasion.

You can wear lots of things, but wearing a warm smile far outweighs the latest fashion. Sound dorky? So be it. It's just the plain and simple truth. A smile tells others you are friendly, approachable, confident, kind, and joyful. Share the joy that Jesus gives—put on a smile and wear it all day!

7

THE COLORFUL INFLUENCE

Color was God's idea. He must have had a blast the day he created it. Test yourself to see what you know about color and *you*!

True or False Quiz

_____ Certain shades make your natural beauty dazzle.

_____ Your skin seems to glow in some colors but appears drained in others.

_____ Discovering what colors work best with your natural coloring will give you a great new sense of presence and confidence.

_____ The idea of certain colors looking better on you than others is a valid theory.

_____ It's a proven fact that color can affect feelings.

_____ Your best colors will brighten your skin and accent your eyes.

_____ Correct colors will direct attention to you rather than to the color itself.

_____ The color theory is divided into four "seasons": winter, summer, spring, and autumn.

_____ Your color season is not related to the season of the year you were born.

_____ Your color season is determined by your skin, eye, and hair coloring—not the season you like the best.

_____ Knowing your best colors can help you weed out clothes that just never looked right on you.

_____ Color can create visual illusions in dressing: lighter colors attract and reflect light, making areas appear larger, whereas darker tones absorb light, causing areas to appear smaller.

_____ You may look great in colors you've never worn before.

Flip to page 94 to get your test results.

The Season Thing

Like I said, color was God's idea. And he lavishly splashed it into four seasons—winter, summer, spring, and autumn. Years ago, a theory was developed that determined some colors look better on us than others. And when we wear those colors, they help us look and feel our best. Let's explore that theory!

When determining your color season, work with the natural, God-given color of your skin, eye, and hair coloring, though the bottom line always comes back to your skin tone.

The tone of your skin comes from three pigments that are present in all skins in differing amounts: melanin (brown), carotene (yellow), and hemoglobin (blue/red). Skins with more hemoglobin have bluish-pink, or cool, undertones. Those with more carotene and melanin have yellowish, or warm, undertones. The special combination of these pigments in your skin gives you unique coloring. Your undertone doesn't change, so the same set of colors will always look good on you.

Winter and Summer

If you have a blue-pink undertone to your skin, you'll look best wearing cool colors. The cool-color categories are further divided into two seasons: Winter and Summer. These two are sister seasons. They contain a range of shades that work to complement each other.

Winters look best in clear tones and dramatic contrasts. In the wintertime, have you noticed how white snow contrasts against the dark bark of empty trees that are outlined by a clear blue sky? This is a typical scene and explains the Winter color scheme. A Winter's best colors are the true primaries—very red, lemon yellow, and sky blue—as well as black, white, gray, icy pastels, true navy, royal blue, shocking pink, deep emerald, and fuchsia. Winter glam girls should avoid browns, rusts, orange, and other spicy earth tones. Winter skin tones are porcelain, snowy cream, rose beige, light to dark olive, or black. Hair colors are light to dark brown, charcoal, reddish black, blue-black, or white. Eye colors are deep blue, dark brown, or gray-green. Rebecca St. James and Ginny Owens are strong Winters!

Summer colors have the same undertones as Winter but with a softer touch—less contrast and more pastels. This season is truly in full bloom. Alive tones like lavender, plum, mauve raspberry, blue-green, and soft white, and cool pastels like pink, mint, and clear yellow are especially great for Summer glam girls. Summer skin tones are fair, pinkish, pale beige, rose-toned beige, or light olive. Hair colors are light to dark brown, ash-blond, or gray. Eye colors are gray-blue, gray-green, aqua, or soft hazel. Natalie Grant and Tammy Trent fit Summer to a T!

Winters and Summers can intermix colors and still be enhancing to the skin tone. It's when they get into warm seasons that their skin appears dull rather than dynamic!

Spring and Autumn

B.A.B.E.s with yellow undertones to their skin wear warm colors. It makes sense, then, that warm colors are colors with a yellow-gold cast to them. If you mixed yellow paint to the primary colors, you would create the warm season's color palette. Spring and Autumn are sister seasons in the warm category.

Spring's palette of clean, fresh, warm tones would include colors like peach, apricot, coral, orange-red, ivory, camel, medium brown, warm or yellowed navy, purple, aqua, yellow-green, and warm turquoise. Spring's skin tones are creamy ivory, peach beige, or warm beige. Hair colors are light to dark blond, strawberry blond, golden brown, or copper. Eye colors are blue-green, topaz, aqua, golden brown, golden green, or hazel. Bethany Dillon and Joy Williams are Spring B.A.B.E.s!

Autumn is the most vivid season. Leaves are turning bright orange, deep rust, and shades of browns and yellows. These underlying tones make up the Autumn color palette. The best tones for Autumn people begin with the spicy earth tones—a full range of brown, nutmeg, rust, cinnamon, burnt orange, bronze, terra-cotta, olive, army green, teal blue, deep periwinkle, beige, camel, salmon, tomato red, and pumpkin. Steer clear of royal blue, deep purple, and hot pink—these cool colors won't jazz up an Autumn's look! Autumn's skin tones are golden, ivory, peach, warm beige, copper cast, or chocolate. Hair colors are brunette with gold or red highlights, golden blond, red, or auburn. Eye colors are dark brown, golden green, hazel, or turquoise. Autumn's undertones are the same as her sister season, Spring, yet Autumn's colors are more intense. Brio Girl 2000 Lisa Velthouse and author Shannon Kubiak Primicerio are definite Autumns! (Hey, check their websites to see if you agree: www.lisavelthouse.com and www.shannonkubiak.com.)

Which season best describes you? _____
Keep reading to see if you're right!

Glam Tip: Bottom line: know if you have cool or warm undertones. This lets you choose colors from a broader range. For example, if you are cool, you can choose colors from the Summer *and* Winter seasons. Some colors may make you look better than others, but as long as they are cool, your appearance will glow like the glam girl you are!

Test Results: Did you guess it? All the answers in the color quiz are TRUE!

Anyone Can Wear Any Color?

Did you notice that some very similar colors were mentioned under different seasons? This may seem contradictory, but it's not. The key to this whole color theory and making it work is this: you can wear any color. You just need to wear the correct shade and intensity of that color for your skin tone! If an Autumn person says she can't wear yellow, she's wrong. It just has to be a golden yellow, whereas Summer's yellow is a clear lemon yellow. Using green as an example, see how the shade and intensity varies for each season. Winter's green is deep emerald, Summer's is blue-green, Spring's is yellow-green, and Autumn's is olive. All of the seasons can wear green in their own special shade. This is a very important key to remember.

Staying with colors within your season is great. I just hope you won't feel restricted to those colors only. Expand into your sister season, staying within your undertone range of cool or warm.

Identify Your Best Colors

Now let's make it all about you! Here are some tests and tips for discovering your coloring and pinpointing your season. Of course, having a professional color analysis done by a qualified color consultant is a big help too!

First, stare at your skin. Study the tones that make up your unique coloring. Do you see cool rosy and pink tones in your cheeks? Are your lips naturally ruby? Perhaps you see more warm yellow tints with an ivory cast. Any freckles? Is your lip color more on the beige side? Which descriptions best fit you? From the descriptions given in the previous sections, which hair and eye color characterize you?

Second, gather a few props. You will need a wide range of solid-colored fabrics like shirts, scarves, towels, or felt squares, or large paint samples—anything with color. Remove all of your makeup. Sit next to a big window that lets in lots of natural light. Place a mirror in front of you and, one at a time, drape the colored fabric over your shoulder and under your chin. Watch the effects the colors have on your skin's appearance. Those that make your skin glow and your eyes sparkle are for you!

Third, do the lipstick test. Enter the lipstick contest as suggested by Carole Jackson, author of the popular color book *Color Me Beautiful.* Try these four lipstick colors, one at a time, and see which makes you look best. Shocking pink represents the Winter season, pastel pink the Summer season, peach the Spring season, and burnt orange the Autumn season. The perfect color is your winning season. Which color looks best on you? Jot it here: _____

If you are still unsure, try comparing your skin tones to someone who already knows her season. How do you measure up? Lighter, darker, more ivory, more olive?

Glam Tip: What's most important is that you have a definite idea of your skin undertones—either cool or warm. Go to www.colormebeautiful.com to help train your eye to see the differences in color. The site is geared toward women older than forty, but here's the deal: the glam makeup is marked warm, cool, and neutral (okay for both). You can see the differences!

Color has the ability to add so much to your appearance and your life! It's also fun to play around with. Discover what color combinations are best for you. Then use these colors to add a splash of brightness to your wardrobe, your mood, and your world. Wear your colors in fullest confidence that you look dazzling in them.

ANDREA'S ADVICE

Because color affects your skin's appearance, the colors you wear next to your face and on your face itself are important. For instance, say your fave sweater is not in your season; go buy (or make) a scarf that *is* in your season and wrap it around your neck. Get the idea? Your makeup colors are an even bigger deal! Choose eye shadow, blush, lip color, and nail colors that are within your season's range of shades.

8

BUILDING a HEALTHIER BOD

You hear it in the classroom, the church pews, and while cruisin' the mall: "Your rear is great in those jeans." "You dropped twelve pounds—that's so cool!" "You look so much thinner—I know everyone will notice."

Compliments. Oh, not about patience or kindness or great grades. Not about how to encourage a mutual friend or how to get along better with parents or what was taught at Sunday school. Compliments center on the body. In fact, they just seep into regular ol' conversation: "I had two desserts last night, and now my jeans barely fit." "I went over my carb limit today." "I can't eat chips—one taste and I'll devour the whole bag." "Do you know how many calories are in that?" "I had too many fat grams yesterday, so I worked out for an hour last night." "I'm skipping lunch today."

On and on. Should we praise our friends when they lose weight? Encourage them to be thinner? Envy them when their new bod wins them attention from guys? Or should we challenge ourselves to bring up topics that don't center around food, fat, and jeans that won't fasten?

Our society's phobia of fat has us craving thinness and clinging to the scale in hopes of reaching some obscure, unattainable "ideal" weight. But ideal according to whom? If you've been checking out the B.A.B.E. Book series, then you can predict what I'll say—the "ideal" is according to the unrealistic beauty standards that have been created by the media and entertainment moguls. We see thin, trim, lean-and-mean models, actresses, and entertainers. (If they're *not* lean, everyone will tell them!) The fat-free body is put up on a pedestal as a prized possession, something to be achieved and worshipped.

Excessive calorie counting, skipping meals, restricting foods, or fixating on fat—none of these is the right way to go about building a healthier body. It's not about being Miss Skinny Minnie. Bottom line—it's all about health. A healthy body is what will help you be all that you were created to be. It will give you the energy, creativity, and good moods needed to do the cool assignments (adventures) that Jesus has waiting for you—the eternally significant ones that are part of your B.A.B.E. status! Then you can give God and the life he has blessed you with your full attention and dedication.

Besides, your body is God's. You can actually glorify him with it. Don't believe me? Read on.

Haven't you yet learned that your body is the home of the Holy Spirit God gave you, and that he lives within you? Your own body does not belong to you. For God has bought you with a great price. So use every part of your body to give glory back to God.

1 Corinthians 6:19–20 TLB

Choosing to eat foods with power-packed nutrients will give you energy, mental alertness, strength, and excitement to do the God-glorifying things you're called to do. Things like being able to concentrate during classes; doing service projects for your family, neighbors, or community on Saturdays (instead of sleeping the day away); being in a good mood; praying with earnestness; and having the

The scale shows a number, but that number is not your overall health score. Being thin does not necessarily mean you are healthy.

strength to endure one more grueling track practice or violin lesson. God has great plans for you—lots of things he wants you to do for him—to be his hands and feet on planet Earth. And it's nutrition that can make a difference. Know the vitamin, mineral, caloric, fiber, fat, protein, sugar, and carbohydrate contents of the stuff you put in your mouth so that you can chow down on what's best—on what will make you *feel* your best so you can *be* your best.

Take advantage of opportunities to study nutrition. Is it worth your time? Yes! You eat every day (you better, anyway), so nutritional facts will be something you will use every single day for the rest of your life. You are worth the investment!

Plus, did you notice what else the Corinthians verse says about your body? It's the home of the Holy Spirit—you're his temple! Let's give him a great place to live by taking care of our bodies. The first step to doing that is to eat right!

Face the Facts

Wanting to look fit and feel good is a major motivator, but only when we want to do it because we care about these bods that God has given to us, *not* when it's because we think we will be more popular or more appealing! That's a rotten trap to get caught in! Tons of teen girls have bought into that lie and have fallen prey to the pitfalls of dangerous dieting, which can lead to eating disorders.

Let's start to turn the tide by looking at what is true!

The Facts

The average fourteen-year-old girl is 5′3″ and weighs 110 to 122 pounds. (She isn't 5′8″ and doesn't weigh 100 pounds!)

By the age of eighteen, the average girl is 5′4½″ and weighs 128 to 135 pounds. Her taller friends will average from 130 to 170 pounds.

The average American woman is 5′4″, weighs 146 pounds, and wears clothing in a size

You can find solid info on vitamins, minerals, and healthy eating, among other things, at www.prevention.com.

12! Over thirty-five million women in our country wear over
size 16.

Those, girl, are the facts. That is reality. That is what is true. The
females we see in the beauty and entertainment industry are not—I
repeat—*are not* the norm! If we compare ourselves to them, we will
always be unhappy with the way we look. Don't let it happen to
you! Plant your feet on solid ground, not shifting sand.

Are you tracking with me on this stuff? Perhaps this illustration
will help. Just like gas is fuel to a car, food is fuel to your body. If
you put water in you car, will it run? No! If you use diesel fuel
when your car needs unleaded, will it run? Yes, but not very well.
What will happen if you fill your tank with premium unleaded? If
will purr like a kitten!

It's the same way with your body! If you don't feed it at all, will
it run? No! You need calories—calories equal energy! If you feed it
things like fries (grease), burgers (high-fat red meat that clogs the
arteries to your heart), donuts (empty calories), candy bars (sugar),
and sodas (chemicals and carbonation), will it run? Yes, but how will
you feel? Tired, sluggish, depressed, unable to concentrate! Some of
you are having a hard time paying attention in class, and it's not just
because your teacher is boring. You're eating the wrong things!

If you choose foods that are power-packed with vitamins, minerals, enzymes, amino acids, and all the healthy stuff you need,
you will feel good and perform at your peak. You will feel more
motivated and alert. Why would you pass that up?

Pause to sit prayerfully before your heavenly Father. Are you
willing to make changes in your eating so you can present him with
a healthier body, a toned-up temple, and a ministry tool? Write your
response as a prayer: _____

_____

_____

_____

_____

_____

Content Consciousness

Let me say this up front—please don't become a compulsive counter! It's unbalanced to be the girl who always refuses to have a piece of birthday cake with the family or calculates the exact number of calories and fat grams in everything that enters her mouth. It's also annoying to everyone around. Still, there are definite benefits to keeping track of nutrients, and knowing the content of what you slip through your lips will work to your benefit when choosing healthy foods. So will keeping track of nutrients.

Knowing which foods are low or high in calories will tell you which foods to eat more of and which ones to eat less of. The same is true for fat grams and fiber content. You will probably be surprised at the info you'll learn about many of your favorite foods. Some of the best foods for you, such as fruits, vegetables, and grains, are low in calories and fat and high in fiber. However, just because something has fewer calories or fat grams doesn't mean it's healthy. Big puffy marshmallows are only twenty-three calories each. Will they build a strong body? No!

If you want to track the value of what you eat, head to Barnes & Noble to pick up a booklet (or go to www.my-calorie-counter.com) that lists calories, fat grams, fiber content, carbs, proteins, and major nutrients (vitamins A, B, C, D, and E; minerals such as calcium, iron, sodium, folic acid, and zinc). Every day for one week, write down everything you eat and drink (including snacks). Make one column each for calories, fat, protein, carbs, and fiber. Use the

Did you know there can be big differences in the number of calories, fat, and fiber in the same food prepared in different ways? For example, one medium-sized apple with the skin on has 80 calories, 0 fat grams, and 3.7 grams of fiber. One cup of sweetened applesauce has 195 calories, 0 fat grams, and 1.5 grams of fiber. One cup of apple juice has 117 calories, 0 fat grams, and 0.2 grams of fiber. A slice of apple pie (1/8 of a 9-inch pie) has 300 calories, 15 fat grams, and 1.0 grams of fiber. Quite a difference, huh?

booklet to hunt down the stats of each item consumed. Add up the total for each day. On a daily basis, the average needs for a teen are as follows: calories 2100–2400; fat 70–80 grams; fiber 28–38 grams; protein 78–90 grams; vitamin C 60 milligrams; calcium 1200 milligrams.*

What do you conclude at the end of the week? Do you need more fiber? Do you need fewer calories but more fat grams? (Fat is not an enemy—the facts on fat are coming up.) Add more of what you need to your daily diet!

Do the Math

One pound equals 3500 calories. To *lose* one pound a week, drop 500 calories a day from your total. Multiply 500 calories a day times seven days in a week for a total of 3500 calories, or one pound. Never eat fewer than 1200 calories a day because doing so keeps your body from burning off calories efficiently—just the opposite of what you want. Plus, losing slowly helps to keep it off. Fast weight-loss methods are rarely lasting. Too many girls set unreachable goals for themselves and then get depressed when they don't reach them. Why do that to yourself? A pound a week is sensible. (Increasing exercise is a must too! More on this coming up!)

To *gain* one pound a week, add 500 calories a day to your total intake. Make them nutrient-dense calories—don't go hog-wild eating fries, milk shakes, or candy bars! You'll gain weight, but you won't be building a strong, healthy body. Couple your healthy eating with a light weight-lifting program and low-impact aerobics like walking. Make the weight gain count!

Think you have ten or more pounds to shed? Have a chat with your family doc before you get started.

What is your *get-real* weight? Dr. Phil says, "It is the weight that is 'right' for you—a stable, comfortable weight. It is the weight at which you look good, feel good, and lovingly accept yourself from the inside out."**

*Jean A. T. Pennington and Judith S. Douglass, *Bowes & Church's Food Values of Portions Commonly Used*, 18th ed. (Philadelphia: JB Lippincott, 2004).
**Dr. Phil McGraw, *The Ultimate Weight Solution* (New York: Free Press, 2004), 9.

Q: "All my friends say I'm too thin and need to gain weight, yet I am small boned and eat practically all the time. Plus, I love eating healthy. Any hints?"

A: No matter what you weigh, eating healthy is vital! Yet keep in mind that the healthiest foods like veggies, fruits, and grains (rice, pasta, and oatmeal) are also the lowest in calories and fat grams. In your case it would be wise to throw some raw almonds, organic peanut or almond butter, and protein bars or shakes into your diet. Use a little butter on your baked potato or add a small slice of cheese to your lunch. You can even drink a yummy chocolate Carnation Instant Breakfast or Boost during the day to provide extra nutrition. This would not be a meal substitute but would be a meal addition.

Don't let your friends' teasing get to you. Just remind them that God is the one who chose to make you small boned. Then smile!

Glam Tip: What? Dark chocolate is *good* for you? According to a recent CNN report (though not supported by some medical associations), dark chocolate contains flavonoids that help the heart and antioxidants that fight certain diseases. It's still high in sugar and fat, but it wins out over white or milk chocolate.*

*CNN.com, July 19, 2005.

Q: "No offense to my aunt, but over the years I've watched her gain and lose weight—over and over! It's like a weird cycle. How can I avoid doing this in my own life?"

A: In my opinion, there are three basic things you can do that will affect your weight now and in the future.

First, educate yourself on nutrition. Head to a bookstore and feast your eyes on the latest info about food. The Internet will work too! Please understand I'm saying educate yourself not on various diets but on food content such as vitamins, carbohydrates, fiber, protein, fats, sodium, calories, and so on. Going on and off diets can mess up metabolism, and eventually the body refuses to lose an ounce.

*Nancy Clark, *Nancy Clark's Sports Nutrition Guidebook: Eating to Fuel Your Active Lifestyle* (Champaign, IL: Leisure Press, 1990).

**Girls, I just wanted you to know that my friend Tricia Bland, who is a super athlete, a certified personal trainer, a registered dietician, the owner of L.E.A.N. Consulting, and the maker of awesome homemade biscotti, shared her expertise in chapters 8 and 9. She rocks.

Second, learn how to cook. Shocking, huh? I realize our culture is all about a grab-it-and-go lifestyle; however, many drive-through foods or unwrap-and-zap foods lack necessary nutrients. Besides, lots of these foods are the cause of Americans packing on the pounds. Learn how to hard-boil an egg, steam fresh veggies, broil fish, create your own whole-wheat pizza crust, grow a small herb garden for use in seasoning your recipes, and so on! Trust me, it's way better to learn this stuff while you're still living at home.

Third, make up your mind that a heart-pumping exercise must be part of your daily to-do list if you want to maintain your weight and build a healthy body. God made your body to move, so choose to be active—it pays off.

Andrea's Do-It List

Do hydrate, hydrate, hydrate! Your body is 60 percent water,* so it needs six to ten cups a day. Choose filtered or distilled water when possible. Flavored waters are good too—still better than a soda!

Do become a label reader! Avoid eating processed foods or anything containing hydrogenated oils, trans fatty acids, or nitrates (mostly in meats). Go as natural as possible.

Do ignore crazy fad diets. It seems as if each month every magazine comes out with a new "no-fail" diet plan. There's the water diet, the grapefruit diet, the hot dog diet, the soup-only diet—they are endless. Ignore them.

Do check into proven weight-loss programs (not fad diets) that teach you how to eat healthy as a lifestyle—not just for a few weeks until your willpower runs out and you quit! Weight Watchers (www.weightwatchers.com) excels at this, and hey, if Fergie does it, it's got to be a royal way to go!

Do take time to think about what you are eating. Chew, taste, swallow—enjoy! Know when you are full. Then stop eating.**

Beauty Bonus with Bethany Dillon: "I have what I call 'traveling zits.' I get them on the road from recycled air in the airplanes and from eating too much grease. I do my best to cut out the grease by eating lean meats, fresh veggies, and lots of fruit. Plus, I take vitamins and drink tons of water instead of sodas."

Andrea's Don't-Do-It List

Don't take diet pills. They claim to curb your appetite, but a large glass of water or herbal tea before you eat will do the same thing.

Don't take water pills (diuretics). They can interfere with your natural body functions and may cause dehydration.

Don't turn to food when you are mad or sad. Using foods to feed your emotional hunger will not solve a thing. Food is a false, temporary high. Okay, it feels great at the time, but the healthiest way to handle an emotional hunger is not with a mega hot fudge sundae! Use what I call "talk therapy." We all need to talk out things that happen in our lives, whether good or bad. We all need to share our thoughts and feelings with someone else. Holding it all in is not the answer. All of life's situations are easier to handle when you get them "outside" yourself through talking. Confide in a special friend, parent, or youth leader. If you feel you don't have a friend to share with, remember you do have a friend in Jesus. He is your heavenly confidant who is there waiting—anytime, anywhere. He wants you to share what is troubling your heart. Go ahead—talk out loud, talk silently, or write in a journal. He can hear you any way. Then be sure you listen for him to respond!

Don't skip meals! You will only end up eating more at the next meal by pushing back your hunger clock. Eating and even drinking water turns up your calorie-burning motor, known as your metabolism. Your body will burn off calories evenly if it's fed proper food on a regular basis. If you don't eat for a day or two, you're fooling yourself. When your body has been deprived of food, the next time you eat it will store all the calories you take in. You don't end up any further ahead.

Healthy How-Tos for Your Bod

1. *Follow the FDA Food Pyramid.* Use the pyramid to evaluate whether you're eating the right foods and the right amount of them to give your body the fuel it needs to function at its best! No need to count calories or fat grams when you let the pyramid be your guide. Eating a variety of foods each day (and taking a multivitamin) will help you get the healthy stuff your body needs! Create your own personalized plan at www .mypyramid.gov.

Check out the FDA Food Pyramid at www.mypyramid.gov.

2. *Fruits and veggies.* Here's the key to healthy cell development and higher energy levels: eat like Adam and Eve! Think garden. Think orchard. Eat two to four fruits and three to five veggies daily. Yes, a glass of juice counts as one serving. Why get caught saying, "I could have had a V8"?

Stick with raw fruits and veggies—as in uncooked and loaded with living enzymes! Cooking fruits and veggies tends to zap the nutrients right out of them, though they're still a better choice than a cupcake or a bag of corn chips! Sprinkle zesty seasonings on that steamed broccoli or cauliflower or dip raw carrots in low-fat dressing if doing so makes them more appetizing. (Other things like raw nuts are great too.)

Think color! Look at what you're about to eat. Do you see shades of orange, red, deep green, yellow, purple, and blue? The more variation of color, the more nutritious the food. And no, I'm not talking Skittles or M&M's!

3. *Go for the grains.* Treat yourself to six to eleven servings per day! A serving would be one slice of whole grain (wheat, rye, barley) bread; a half cup of cooked brown rice,

The Best of the Best

Below are a few of the most nutritionally charged foods that you need to work into your eating as often as possible. They are bursting with essential nutrients and fancy sounding things like antioxidants, phytonutrients, beta-carotene, omega-3 fatty acids, and a whole lot more! Plus, they have been found to help prevent certain cancers and other illnesses. Ready?

Blueberries! Broccoli! Tuna! Skim Milk! Sweet potatoes! Avocados! Carrots! Spinach! Garlic! Salmon! Soy products!

oatmeal, or pasta; a half cup of whole grain, nonsugared cereal (add honey to sweeten up cereals). Now you're getting the carbohydrates and fiber—a must for keeping food moving through the intestines at a regular pace. You need it for a better you!

4. ***Build strong bones.*** It's easy with bone-strengthening dairy products that are full of calcium—very vital for your growing body! Try 1 cup skim or calcium-fortified soy milk, ½ cup nonfat yogurt, ½ cup 2 percent cottage cheese, and reduced-fat cheese (limit cheese to an occasional treat due to its high fat, artery-clogging content). Oranges, broccoli, and Total cereal have some calcium too. Remember—1200 milligrams per day.

5. ***Power-packed protein.*** Pump up those muscles with power-packed protein! Steer clear of red, packaged, or processed meats (I'm talking hot dogs here!). Choose grilled or broiled chicken, turkey, fish (a serving is about the size of your fist), or other super sources of protein like beans, peas, nuts such as raw almonds, eggs, soy products, yogurt smoothies, and protein drinks or bars.

6. ***Friendly fat options.*** Those high-fat treats that make us weak in the knees can also weaken our bodies! Yes, we must have fat in our diet for certain vitamins to be assimilated in our bodies and for our hormones to function properly. Do you know any girl who

Some foods need to be cooked for safety reasons, but if they don't, go raw. It's the health- iest way to eat!

Cruciferous Crunch

You might have to make yourself do this one, but choose to work this specific group of veggies into your eating each week. Crucifers are plants that have flowers with petals in the shape of a cross and long, narrow seed pods. They are known for helping detoxify the body and attacking cancer-causing chemicals. Here's the lineup: cabbage, broccoli, cauliflower, brussels sprouts, collard and mustard greens, turnip greens, and radishes. Excited, aren't you?

Q: "I know that I don't need to eat meat more than once a day, but I don't know any good veggie sandwich recipes. Do you?"

A: Congratulations! Choosing to limit your meat intake to once a day is a very healthy choice as long as you include other sources of protein like cheese and beans. Give these recipes a try.

California Veggie Wrap
1 tortilla
Spicy reduced-fat mayo or mustard
1 slice of cheese (part-skim mozzarella or reduced-fat cheddar)
1/8 of an avocado
Shredded lettuce
Veggies (try cucumber, zucchini, carrots, corn, fresh peppers)

Spread mayo or mustard on tortilla. Add cheese, lettuce, avocado, and veggies. Fold $\frac{1}{4}$ of tortilla toward center to secure ingredients, then roll tortilla as you "wrap in" the veggies!

Spicy Bean Burgers
1 15 oz. can of spicy chili beans
1 cup plain bread crumbs
1/4 cup finely chopped onion
1 slightly beaten egg
Dash of Tabasco or ground pepper (optional)

In a bowl, mash undrained beans. Add bread crumbs, onion, and egg. Mix well. Make 4 or 5 patties. Cook for 6 to 8 minutes over medium heat in a nonstick skillet sprayed with cooking spray. Turn after 3 minutes. Serve in whole wheat buns with your favorite toppings.

has cut so much fat from her diet that her period has stopped? That's incredibly unhealthy! So choose monounsaturated or "healthy" fats like olive oil for yummy salad dressing and cooking, avocados to spice up your veggie sandwich or make guacamole, and almonds on your fruit cup! Limit other fats to very small servings like one or two teaspoons per day of butter, mayo, cream cheese, or sour cream. Learning to love mustard instead of mayo—or ketchup or BBQ sauce (due to sugar)—is perfect! Butter Buds® and Brummel & Brown® are flavorful butter options—and no trans fats!

7. *Tempting tasties.* Sweeten up foods with honey, fruit spreads, fruit juice, or other natural sweeteners such as fructose (available at health food stores). Forget the artificial sweeteners. And don't make cookies, candies, ice cream, or cake items a daily habit! Remember, we're choosing healthier foods. Yes, you can have desserts! Try a bowl of fresh strawberries trickled with honey and wheat germ (a vitamin E boost), or mashed raspberries on a half cup of frozen yogurt, or sugar-free chocolate pudding with a squirt of whipped cream. You can make your own juice pops by putting chunks of watermelon in a blender—puree, then pour the liquid into cups to put in the freezer (add sticks when half frozen).

8. *Sensible snacks.* When you get the munchies, go for smart snacks like smoothies made with low-fat yogurt (not ice cream!), fresh fruit, pretzels, *baked* chips and salsa, rice cakes, air-popped popcorn with cheese flavoring, fruit-juice (100 percent) bars, fat-free pudding, sugar-free Jell-O, fruit leathers, hummus (chickpeas), or carrot sticks. It's best to make your snacks a combo of carbohydrates and protein. It will help maintain your energy level and keep your tummy happy. Try refried beans wrapped in a small whole-wheat tortilla, raw veggies dipped in nonfat sour cream mixed with salsa, an apple with a few slices of cheese, low-fat cottage cheese spread on whole-wheat crackers, or hummus spread on pita bread triangles.

9. *Perfect picks.* When you're pulling up to that drive-through window, choose grilled chicken over burgers, veggie over bean bur-

Many foods are available in three forms: fresh, frozen, or canned. Fresh is always best, then frozen, and lastly canned (they're packed with sodium).

ritos, chicken soft taco over beef burrito, pancakes over breakfast sandwiches, veggie over triple meat pizza, juice or iced tea over soda, baked potato over fries—get the picture? Check your local bookstore or the websites of your fave restaurants for fast-food nutritional guides.

10. *Stay balanced.* The Bible encourages us to do things in moderation. Don't go overboard being so strict with your eating that life loses its fun. Likewise, avoid eating anything you want anytime you want it! You are working toward a healthier you that will have a happier attitude and outlook on life. Eating well and doing regular exercise will help you get there. Get some great recipes at www .deliciousdecisions.org!

Q: "I am deep into the first semester of school, and I come home tired and hungry. What can I eat that will pick me up?"

A: Try reduced-fat peanut butter (fresh ground organic is best) on whole wheat crackers. Add a squirt of honey if you need something sweet. You can also whip up one of these luscious lifters that will reenergize your brain and pep you up before you dive into that pile of homework!

Peaches 'n' Cream Concoction
Put one cut-up peach (fresh or frozen) into a blender. Add $\frac{1}{2}$ cup peach yogurt, $\frac{3}{4}$ cup low-fat milk, and several ice cubes. Puree until smooth. Bottoms up!

Chocolate Banana Almond Delight
Put $\frac{1}{4}$ cup cold water and $\frac{1}{2}$ cup slivered almonds into a blender and puree until almonds are finely chopped. You may need to stop the blender and use a spatula to push the almonds to the bottom blade. Add one sliced banana (you can put it in the freezer for an hour if you want an extra chilly smoothie), $\frac{1}{2}$ cup low-fat milk, 2–3 tablespoons chocolate syrup, and a handful of ice. Mix at high speed until creamy. Add more milk if it's too thick for you. Totally yummy!

Steer-Clear Substances

Since we're talking about nutrition and caring for our bodies, I want to make you aware of three nutrition and beauty robbers that dance around in costumes of fun: drugs, alcohol, and cigarettes.

Drugs and alcohol strip the body of nutrients, dehydrate the skin, and have lasting ill effects. Smoking cigarettes or marijuana will quickly age your skin by drying it—though the deadliest damage is caused to the lungs.

Drugs affect your body in other ways also, many that we are only now discovering. They can alter your thinking, alter your emotions, and definitely damage your health. Drugs literally invade every part of your body, and just like alcohol and tobacco, they are addictive. They change your body chemistry, making you dependent upon the drug. Playing with social drugs such as marijuana, cocaine, and crack is not the kind of game you can just walk away from. You must choose for yourself to play or not to play. **No one can make you get into the game.** Alcohol, which is very available but very harmful, is one of the **major causes of death among teenagers**. It's not something you want to fool with. It's one of the enemy's tools to destroy healthy young adults.

Most teens who experiment with drugs and alcohol do so because of peer pressure or problems at home. You must decide what your response to drugs, alcohol, and cigarettes will be *before* they are presented to you. They're *not* cool. They're a trap. You can get out, but you can avoid getting into the trap altogether if you choose to say no beforehand, then follow through if you have moments when the pressure to participate stares you in the face. Choose to follow the Lord's best rather than give in to pressure from your friends. Friends? Those who get others trapped in drugs or drinking are not friends.

ANDREA'S ADVICE

Know your stuff! A carbohydrate is a source of calories and the primary fuel required for your muscles and brain. Protein is a source of calories and is essential for the growth and repair of your muscles, organs, red blood cells, and hair, and for making hormones. A fat is a source of calories that are stored and function as an energy (fuel) reserve. Fiber is the part of plants that humans cannot digest. These substances add bulk to your diet that allows for regular bowel functions.

Seeing the damaging effects of drugs and alcohol on the lives of so many people has convinced me that our loving God wants us to steer clear of these harmful indulgences.

> Don't be drunk with wine, because that will ruin your life. Instead, let the Holy Spirit fill and control you.
>
> Ephesians 5:18 NLT

> Wine produces mockers; liquor leads to brawls. Whoever is led astray by drink cannot be wise.
>
> Proverbs 20:1 NLT

I believe this holds true no matter what your age. I don't believe that once you turn eighteen or twenty-one it's okay to party hardy. I urge you to be strong and say no to smoking, drugs, and alcohol, even if it means losing some friends or having a goody-goody reputation. In the end you will win. You will do your body a lot of good. After all, your body's a holy temple. Treat it like one.

Glam Tip: Cigarette smoke inhaled directly or secondhand is a definite beauty buster. It's tough on skin, hair, teeth, breath, lungs, and fingernails. It can taint a girl's reputation and testimony. It's not cool. It's not sexy. It can't make you skinny.

A Different Kind of Food

We've covered feeding the physical part of you. But what about feeding the other part of you that's equally important—your spiritual self? Yes, that needs nutrition too. Each of us has a spiritual nature that hungers for God. Some describe it as a God-shaped hole that only God himself can fill.

Many people get wrapped up in the wrong things in their attempts to nourish the spiritual hunger inside of them: overeating, drinking alcohol, taking drugs, having sex, watching tons of TV, spending every extra second on their cell or IM or with their iPod wired to their ears, burying themselves in studies or work. Worse yet is when they experiment with cults, witchcraft, Eastern religions, or Satanism. They know they need something. They are searching for something to satisfy them, to give them security and purpose. But they can't figure out or admit what their need really is. It is God!

Let's look at a meal for nourishing your spiritual self. The appetizer you should serve your spiritual hunger is Jesus. He must be first! Simply ask him to come and live in your heart. When you do this, you are forgiven, and you become one with God and have peace with him. You are new inside, or born again. Your spirit is what becomes new. Jesus says in John 6:35 that he is the bread of life and that if we have him, we will not be spiritually hungry. Just as we don't eat food just once and then never again, so we must not fill up just once on Jesus and then call it enough. We need to feed on him daily!

You can experience the fruit of the Holy Spirit's characteristics in your life. Here is a refreshing fruit salad in the form of being filled with the Holy Spirit: love, joy, peace, patience, kindness, goodness, faithfulness, gentleness, and self-control. We have these great qualities in us because Jesus lives in us through the Holy Spirit.

Here comes the main entrée, the real meat and potatoes: a healthy helping of the Word of God. This is straight spiritual food that your spirit needs. The Bible is your handbook to life. It teaches you and guides you according to God's will for your life. Jesus said his food was to do the will of his Father God (see John 4:34). The same applies to you. It feeds your spirit to learn and to do God's will.

And now for your spiritual dessert: hanging out with other believers. Finding out what God has done and is doing in others' lives helps your faith grow and nourishes your spirit. Worshipping with others (and alone) is also a sweet experience

"Let your roots grow down into him [Christ] and draw up nourishment from him. See that you go on growing in the Lord, and become strong and vigorous in the truth" (Colossians 2:7 TLB).

that can fulfill you deep down. Listen to the *WOW Worship* CDs and see how your spirit responds!

You are perfectly and completely created with a physical nature and a spiritual nature. Feeding them both guarantees you complete nutrition so you can look, feel, and be your best for the Lord!

9

TOTAL FITNESS

Life sneaks little exercises in on you every day. You automatically tighten your abs and do a sit-up to get out of bed. You give your thighs and calves a miniworkout each time you tackle the stairs. You tone your hamstrings from toe touches every time you bend over to pick up something. Are you reaching up to get a sweater off the top shelf? It's a great stretch!

Contrary to what some girls think, fitness is fun! There are so many types of sports and forms of exercise that becoming fit can also be enjoyable. The options are endless: hiking, biking, skiing, surfing, spinning, kickboxing, Pilates, nailing a home run—all of it counts! Yes, it can be hard work, but the rewards of a healthy, physically fit body are worth every drop of glistening sweat.

Why Work Out?

If I asked ten teen girls why they should work out, nine of the answers would be about weight. That's the wrong focus! One girl could weigh fifteen pounds less than her friend, but that doesn't mean she is in better shape. The bathroom scale does not determine your fitness level. Body weight is not the way to measure fitness. Exercise helps in weight loss, but more important, exercise is for physical fitness. It's about health and body composition on the inside—you know, the condition of your heart, lungs, organs, and cholesterol. And a healthy you is a happier, more energized you! B.A.B.E.s need bods that can use the special abilities and spiritual gifts they have been blessed with. Believe me, you *want* to be in great shape to do all the cool, fun, and eternally significant things God has planned for you. Your body, God's temple, is your engine. So turn on your motor and get in shape!

Here are even more benefits to working out:

Increases cardiovascular fitness (heart and lungs)

Firms up muscle tissue and increases muscle strength

Increases overall body strength

Increases lean muscle mass so your engine runs faster and burns more calories—the more muscle you have, the more calories are burned and the more inches you can lose (muscle tissue uses up more calories per hour than fat)

Increases energy, stamina, and brainpower

Pumps mood-elevating endorphins into the bloodstream

Increases flexibility, coordination, and core balance

Helps toward the prevention of heart disease, osteoporosis, diabetes, and high blood pressure

Relieves stress and pent-up emotions and enhances the immune system

Can ease menstrual cramps

Improves posture

Regulates your circulation and digestive system

Makes a B.A.B.E. feel great

You can't fool your body. It knows the difference between busy work that basically exhausts you and real exercise that eventually energizes you.

A Is for Aerobic

We're going to talk about two kinds of workout: aerobic and nonaerobic. Each kind achieves different results. Most aerobic exercise involves your whole body, thus strengthening and toning your heart, lungs, and major muscle groups. Nonaerobic exercise targets specific muscles to firm, tone, and sculpt. You need *both* for a complete exercise program. Let's start with aerobic.

Aerobic means "air" or "oxygen." This kind of exercise requires an increase in the amount of air you take in and an increase in your heart rate. It will strengthen your heart and lungs and provide overall tone to your large muscles. To get the greatest benefit from aerobic exercise, you need to do it (1) long enough, (2) hard enough, and (3) regularly.

Generally speaking, you should exercise for thirty minutes nonstop. Why? Initially your bod just burns up available "fuel." It takes longer to reach the point where it's burning up "stored fuel." And that's what you want! So you start with two minutes of warm-up, do the thirty, and end with two minutes of cool down (to prevent soreness). Note that I said you must do this *nonstop*! If you quit in the middle of your workout, whether it's to get the door or answer your cell, your heart rate will drop. Allowing interruptions is still better than doing nothing, but you gotta keep going long enough if you want to get great results.

In exercising hard enough, your goal is to keep your heart working continuously at its midpoint *training rate*, which is approximately 80 percent of its *maximum working rate*. You can test your heart rate during your exercise period by checking your pulse. Locate a clock or watch with a second hand. Place your fingers, not your thumb, on your wrist or on the side of your neck to locate your pulse. Count the number of beats you feel in six seconds. Multiply that number by ten. For teens, the average training heart rate is between 160 and 170 beats per minute. If you're below 160, work harder. If you're above 180, slow down. I know you can get your heartbeat over 180

Before beginning an exercise program, have a physical exam by your doctor to eliminate any potential problems that exercise may complicate.

beats per minute, but don't! Let your conversation be your guide: if you are unable to chat it up with your gal pals during your workout, you are working too hard. Yep, you should be huffing and puffing while you're talking but not be breathless.

Now about number three—regular enough! I know you're smart enough to figure this one out! Aerobic or cardio fitness needs to be done four to six times a week.

As your body adjusts to a new amount of physical activity, you can work harder and longer. If your fitness activity hasn't been more than strolling from class to class or going back and forth between the couch and the fridge, simply begin with a brisk walk—start with ten minutes and increase from there. This may be enough to get your heart to its training rate. Don't be embarrassed—every **body** has to start somewhere! Let your pulse and your breathing be your guide.

Choose from walking, jogging, swimming laps, spinning, jumping rope, biking, rollerblading, hiking, cross-country skiing, kickboxing, dancing, or Tae Bo®, or try machines like the treadmill, rower, stair climber, recumbent seat, elliptical, or stationery bike. Remember, these exercises become aerobic when you do them long enough, hard enough, and nonstop. Some (like jumping rope) are more strenuous than others, yet how will you know if you're in your target zone? **By checking your pulse!**

Since aerobic exercise conditions the heart, it is commonly referred to as *cardio fitness.* If someone asks you if you've done your cardio workout today, they are referring to your thirty-minute aerobic workout. So, got cardio? You will if you attempt Tae Bo®, designed by Billy Blanks (www.billyblanks.com).

ANDREA'S ADVICE

Be creative and alternate your routine to keep it fresh and fun. Invite a friend to join you. You don't have to belong to a fitness club to get a good workout—just have a great pair of shoes (with good arch support and heel cushioning) and a positive attitude that helps you make exercise a way of life.

The Nonaerobic Advantage

Nonaerobic exercises, which don't require a heavy intake of air, include things like weight lifting, calisthenics, and isometrics. Each of these focuses on toning, strengthening, and sculpting muscles—one at a time! For example, when you do a sit-up, you are primarily working your abdominal muscles; you aren't doing much for your upper arms. Likewise, side stretches may firm your waistline but your calves aren't getting a whole lot out of the experience. Get it?

Adding Weights

Strength or resistance training is a great way to tone and sculpt your muscles. Just add weights! Adding ankle and wrist weights to your exercises is a great way to begin a light weight-lifting program. Move to three-pound dumbbells from there. Weights are to be used every *other* day. This allows time for the repair and building of the muscles. The results will be well-defined muscle shape and increased muscle mass. No, you won't start looking like a guy if you lift weights, because you don't have all the testosterone they have. The female physique is different from the male physique (as if you hadn't noticed!). Good muscle tone with a touch of definition looks fit and healthy. Weights and resistance are the key!

And so is breathing! Here's the rule: exhale with the effort. In other words, if you are doing bicep curls, you exhale as you bring the weight up toward your shoulder.

To get the complete how-tos on strength training and weight lifting, check out the President's Council

Metabolism is the rate at which your body burns up calories from food and uses them for fuel. The higher it is, the more calories get burned. Metabolism is determined by your eating habits, physical activity, and how much muscle you have. Want to increase it? Eat healthy and exercise daily. Want to decrease it? Jump on the latest fad diet, crash diet, or yo-yo (on again-off again) diet, or be a couch potato. These can mess up your metabolism.

on Physical Fitness and Sports at http://fitness.gov/activelife/pepup/ pepup.html, or see www.familydoctor.org.

The Name Game

Do you like it when someone calls you the wrong name? What about when they refer to you as so-and-so's daughter instead of using your name? Have you ever been called a nickname? Real names work best. And they make sense! Why call your abdominal muscle "tummy muscle"? Get educated and use the real names!

Let's see what you already know. Write the name of the muscle that coordinates with the alphabetical letter. Then check your answers on p. 122. If you get more than ten correct, you rock!

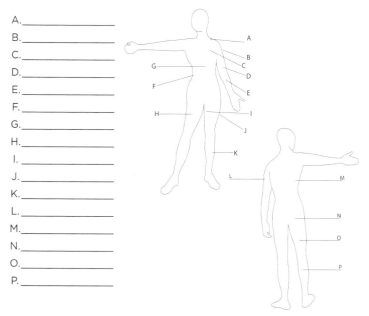

A._____
B._____
C._____
D._____
E._____
F._____
G._____
H._____
I. _____
J._____
K._____
L._____
M._____
N._____
O._____
P._____

The Total-Body Workout

I am providing you with a total-body, target-toning routine with pictures and all. These are basic exercises that will give you a strong foundation. Study and expand from here.* A few things to note:

*Check out pages 131–34 for illustrations of most exercises.

Hold all stretches for about fifteen seconds so the muscles have time to contract and then relax into the stretch and get the full benefit. Stretching gets your body and mind ready to move. It helps reduce muscle tension; increases muscle length, range of motion around your joints, circulation, and your core temperature (warming up); and prepares your body for exercise. Therefore, is it important? **Yes!**

Pulse It means to do minilifts at the end of the exercise. If you're instructed to *pulse it* at the end of your abdominal crunches (sit-ups), stay in the tightened position and do little minilifts or minicrunches. Don't add pulses to your routine until the second week of working out.

The first week of your routine, don't use weights. The next few weeks, use three-pound ones, then gradually increase the weight to build the muscle tissue.

You will need workout shoes, a floor mat (or carpeting), three- and five-pound dumbbells, a stability abs ball, Velcro ankle weights, comfortable clothes, and water so you can hydrate, hydrate, hydrate!

As a general rule, do these exercises (and weight training) every other day, though cardio training (aerobics) can be done four to six times a week.

Don't hold your breath! Exhale or blow out with exertion (effort), inhale on recovery (going back to the original position).

Pilates is the rage on the Hollywood scene and anyone who is serious about getting in shape fast. Ready to try it? Get info at www .easyvigour.net.nz/pilates/HowPilEx .pdf to see how it's done. Then hit www.deniseaustin.com and order her Pilates DVD. In my opinion, she has the most balanced approach to exercise and fitness and is a natural encourager! Once in a blue moon she uses the word *sexy*, but you can ignore that. It's not our goal as B.A.B.E.s!

Beauty Bonus with Jeni Varnadeau: "For me, not only is fitness essential for my physical, mental, and emotional well-being, it's also a fun, creative outlet. I view fitness like painters see their paints and brushes—so many exercise choices and combinations that can be pieced together to make a colorful, exciting workout. I especially like the exercise balance ball (do a few crunches on that thing and you're sore!), hiking, and hip-hop." (Check out www.jenivarnadeau.com.)

Front: A. Trapezius (traps) B. Deltoid (delts) C. Pectorals (pecs) D. Biceps E. Forearm (too many small muscles to name) F. Obliques G. Rectus abdominis (abs) H. Quadriceps (quads) I. Adductors (inner thigh) J. Abductors (outer thigh) K. Tibialis anterior (shin)
Back: L. Triceps M. Latissimus dorsi (lats) N. Gluteus maximus (glutes) O. Hamstrings (hams) P. Gastrocnemius (calf)

Traps and Delts

1. Start with head rolls. Gently bend your chin toward your chest. Slowly roll your head to the right, looking over your right shoulder, then slowly roll your head forward and to the left, looking over your left shoulder. Repeat exercise ten times.

2. For shoulder shrugs, lift your shoulders toward your ears, then slowly roll them to the back, down, forward, and return to the uplifted position. Repeat five times, then reverse the direction.

Triceps and Biceps

3. Start with your arms straight out at shoulder level. Begin making small circles, rotating your arms forward. Gradually enlarge the circles. Do ten circles, then repeat, rotating in the opposite direction. Work up to three sets of ten in each direction.

4. With your arms straight out in front of you, press your palms together with lots of resistance. Hold to the count of three,

Q: "My friends are getting into weights. Do you think weights are a good thing?"

A: Absolutely! Light weight lifting, whether it's with machines or free weights (like dumbbells), provides a great workout for your muscles! But that's not the only benefit. Weight-lifting exercises can increase bone density, therefore making your bones stronger. They also increase your metabolism (the rate that your body burns off calories) and often your sense of balance and your confidence level. Plus, you get a healthier look and feel. When beginning a workout with weights, start with three to five pounds, then increase the weight as your muscles adjust and become stronger. You have to stick with it to see results.

then release. Repeat ten times. This is a great isometric exercise for your biceps and pectorals. To make this exercise effective for your triceps, cross your forearms and turn your hands, palms together. Press five seconds, release. Start with ten and build up.

5. While on the floor, get into the modified push-up position (knees on floor). Your body from the back of your knees to your neck should be flat—don't lift your glutes into the air. Do ten push-ups, working up to three sets of ten.

Lats

6. While standing, raise your arms to shoulder level, placing one forearm on top of the other and making a big square. Pull your arms back as far as you can. Hold for five seconds; return to starting position. Repeat ten times.

7. Lie facedown on the floor, arms extended outward, as if you're flying. Lift your arms, head, and shoulders off the floor. Exhale and blow out for the count of five. Relax. Do not strain your lower back. The pull should be in the upper body area. Begin with five; slowly work up to ten.

While you're still facedown, clasp your hands together behind you and pull, lifting your head and upper body. Exhale for five counts, then relax. Repeat ten times.

Obliques

8. Start with a full stretch, reaching as high as you can. With your hands over your head, bend toward the right for fifteen counts, then the same to the left. Repeat twice.

9. Put your arms straight out to the sides. Stand with your feet shoulder-width apart and bend your knees slightly. Tighten your abs and glutes. Slowly twist from side to side. Twist ten times.

10. Sit on the floor and prop yourself up on your elbows. Keep your left leg straight

If you weigh yourself daily and it freaks you out, stop it. Forget it. Never allow the scale to steal your focus for the day—or your joy!

and your right leg bent. Cross your right knee over your left leg. Stretch and extend to the floor; hold for the count of three. Repeat ten times, then change legs.

Lower Back and Hamstrings

11. Stand with your feet together and exhale while bending forward toward the floor. Don't bounce; just hang there. Relax your lower back into the stretch. Repeat five times.

12. Stand with your feet spread about two feet apart. Bend over, touching your left foot, then center, then right foot. Return to uplifted position. Repeat ten times. For an extra challenge, try walking your hands out on the floor in front of you to stretch the hamstrings and calves. Try keeping your heels on the floor.

13. Hold onto the back of a chair. Extend one leg behind you, then lift and lower it twenty times. On the last lift, hold it up and pulse it ten times. Repeat on opposite leg.

Q: "The backs of my upper arms really jiggle. What can I do to firm them?"

A: You need a good ***triceps toner***. In a typical day, your triceps get very little use, so exercises that target that area are essential. Stand in front of a sturdy chair as if you are going to sit down. Step forward about twelve inches. Lower yourself down and place your hands on the front edge of the chair. Your fingers should be facing forward and your knees should be at a 90 degree angle. Keep your feet on the floor and lower your body until your elbows are at a 90 degree angle. Slowly push yourself back up. Repeat six times. Rest. Repeat. As your triceps begin to firm up and your muscle strength increases, increase the repetitions to ten.

But wait—you're only half done! You always need to ***work the opposite muscles***—in this case, the ***biceps***! Using a heavy soup can, a water bottle, or a three- to five-pound dumbbell, put your elbows against your sides in order to isolate the muscle, then curl the weight toward your shoulder, then back down. Repeat for a total of ten repetitions. Increase the amount of weight and number of repetitions when this is no longer challenging.

Abs: Upper and Lower

Core note: Before you begin each abdominal exercise, tighten your ab muscles as if you were trying to press your belly button toward your spine. Add your arms to the exercise to concentrate on your upper abs. Add your legs to focus on your lower abs.

14. For your upper abs, lie on your back and cross your arms over your chest. Lift your head and shoulders about five inches off the floor. Exhale for a count of three; return to the original position. Repeat ten times, then pulse it ten times on the last one. Add ten repetitions each week.

15. Using your stability ball, lie faceup with knees bent, feet on the floor, the ball hugging the curve of your back (your bottom is right off the edge of the ball). Put your hands behind your neck with elbows straight out. Looking and lifting up toward the ceiling (keeping elbows in), slightly crunch your abs. Do three sets of ten; aim to work up to one hundred.

16. For lower abs, lie on your back, pressing belly button to spine, and lift your legs off the floor twelve inches. Lifting your upper bod, reach toward your toes and pulse it twenty times. Repeat. Work it up to one hundred.

17. While lying on your back, straighten legs, lift them off the floor, and make a scissors motion. Repeat ten times, then relax.

Adductors: Inner Thighs

18. Stand with your feet three to four feet apart, knees bent and hands on the floor. Lunge toward the left, then to the right. Begin slowly in order to stretch, not pull, your muscles. Lunge five times to each side, holding each stretch fifteen seconds.

Get to the core! Core training, or strengthening your abs and lower back (the "core" of your bod), is vital for fabulous fitness. It's the center of your body and therefore *must* be the strongest area—everything extends from your core. Do core fitness three times a week to get fab abs!

19. Lie on your side and do ten leg lifts. Stretch that inner thigh muscle. Roll your hip slightly forward. Point your toe toward the floor and do ten more lifts. This position works on your outer thighs and the backs of your legs.

20. Lie on your back with your legs extended toward the ceiling. Cross them, stretching the outer thigh, then open them, stretching the inner thigh. Support your lower back by placing your hands under your glutes. Repeat ten times.

21. Lie on your left side, supporting yourself with your left forearm. Extend your left leg, bend your right leg, and place your right foot in front of your left knee. Hold your right ankle with your right hand. Lift your left leg. Lower slowly. Repeat twenty times, then pulse it ten. Change sides. Add ankle weights later.

22. Get a pillow or a soft, squeezable ball, like a Nerf ball; place it between your knees and slide down against the side of a wall. Hold for one minute. Repeat three times. Increase the minutes as your muscles begin to shape up from this isometric exercise!

Q: "I'm not as active as I was last summer, and I notice my inner thighs seem 'looser.' Know of a good exercise to help?"

A: Oh, yeah! Here's a toning exercise that will work your thighs and backside. It's even somewhat ladylike—it feels like a cute little curtsy! With your hands on your hips, stand with one foot in front of the other. Slightly turn your feet outward. Lower yourself down into curtsy position, keeping your back straight and heels on the floor. (Yes it's really a squat, but I'm trying to make it seem less athletically charged.) To protect your knees, never let them extend over your toes. Sit back like you're a jockey on a horse—keep your bottom back! As you come back up, purposely squeeze your inner thighs and gluts. Release. Repeat ten times, then switch feet and do ten more. Do this every day and you'll see results!

Abductors: Outer Thighs

23. Sit on the floor with both knees bent to the left. Use your arms to keep you steady. Extend your top leg out to the side, then back in. Repeat ten times, then change sides.

24. Get down on all fours and bring your left knee to your chin. Extend your leg back and up, head lifted. Repeat ten times on each side. Pulse it the last ten times.

Hips and Glutes

25. Now, instead of extending your leg back, lift it to the side, straighten it (point those toes), and return to starting position. Repeat ten times, then change legs. Pulse it! When you get really good at these, add ankle weights.

26. Start in a kneeling position. Hold your arms straight out in front of you, then slowly lean back, tightening your glutes and abs. Do not sit down. Lift back up, then repeat ten times.

27. Lie facedown with your arms at your sides and your forehead on the floor. Lift both legs off the floor and do a quick set of ten scissor kicks. Point those toes! Lower your legs. Repeat.

28. Roll over on your back, arms at your sides, feet about twelve inches apart and directly under your knees. Lift your hips to the ceiling, tightening your glutes. Hold five seconds, and then lower your hips. Repeat twenty times and pulse it on the last one.

Calves and Shins

29. Hold onto the back of a chair or the wall. Lift up on your toes as high as you can. Slowly lower your heels back down to the floor. Repeat ten times.

30. Doing the same toe raises as above, change your toe position to work the inner and outer calves. Turn toes inward and do ten raises. Turn toes outward and do ten raises.

31. Stand on the front edge of a thick book or a step, rise up on the toes, then drop your heels below the book or stair to stretch your calves and Achilles tendon. Repeat ten times.

Whew!

Shake out your whole body. Relax! Pat yourself on the back—you did it!

Measure your progress by the way you feel, not with a

It is possible to have rock-hard abs and still have excess soft tissue on top. Only aerobic or cardio workout attacks the tissue on top of the muscles. That, glam girl, is another reason that a combination of aerobic and nonaerobic exercise is the key to the healthiest you!

scale. Scales can be deceiving. Our body fluids fluctuate daily, and near menstruation time we retain water. The scale will show these changes, and it can be discouraging. A scale is a number, but it does *not* give your percentage of lean muscle mass, fat mass, bone density, or water mass. And all that together determines our weight. Your focus should be on healthy eating and exercising regularly, not on the scale. A healthy body is the goal!

Instead, ask yourself: Do I have more energy? Are my clothes fitting differently as my muscles get longer and leaner? Am I feeling more positive and less stressed as those endorphins get released into my bloodstream? Can I concentrate better? Am I stronger? Do I have to catch my breath after climbing stairs? Am I less worn out at the end of the day? Am I looking forward to my workouts? These are the best ways to measure your *real* progress.

Glam Tip: Make every step count! Get to a sports store, buy a pedometer, clip it to your shoe or belt, and let it track every step you take. The Aerobics and Fitness Association of America challenges us to take 10,000 steps per day! Get started. It will show you if you are active enough or need to turn up the heat!

Firm Up Your Faith

Just like you can work your muscles to firm and strengthen them, you can do the same with your faith! Yet unlike your triceps or abs, your faith doesn't naturally weaken with age—you can keep it strong, active, and alive from now into eternity. Remember, when you leave this earth, your body stays here, but your spirit goes to be with the Lord. (I hope that excites and energizes you.) So, B.A.B.E.s, the effort you put into building your faith is worth the investment of time.

In the Bible, the apostle Paul (the guy who wrote two-

Find a few good reads on health and exercise from the National Strength and Conditioning Association at www.nsca.com. Get exercise ideas at www.fitness.gov, www.easyvigour.net, and www.primusweb.com/fitnesspartner/index.html.

thirds of the New Testament) said to young Timothy, "Train yourself to be godly. For physical training is of some value, but godliness has value for all things, holding promise for both the present life and the life to come" (1 Timothy 4:7–8 NIV). How does godliness begin? By faith!

No one's faith starts out big and strong. Jesus talks about faith beginning very small—the size of a tiny mustard seed (see Matthew 17:20). As that seed is given proper care, it grows into a huge plant. Your faith might start small, but it has big potential. Jesus told his disciples that with even a small amount of faith they could do great things for him. When you live by WWJD and the Bible's teaching, *you* are his disciple too. You can take your faith, grow it, apply it, and watch to see how the Lord will use you. Going on adventures with Jesus is what makes the Christian life exciting! If you think being a follower of Jesus is boring, perhaps you need to get to know him better by studying his Word (the Bible), by talking with him (prayer), and by trusting him with all your personal "stuff." Then watch to see how he responds. These things will stretch your faith.

You can also increase your faith by knowing and believing God's promises. First, know his word: "Faith comes from hearing the message, and the message is heard through the word of Christ" (Romans 10:17 NIV). Take him at his word. You will feel pumped about life. For instance, when you confess your sins, believe that they are forgiven. Then you can live with a clear conscience, and how great that feels! (This is a righteous reason for daily con-

ANDREA'S ADVICE

Before you flop down in front of the TV, do some bends and stretches by picking up clutter and putting it away—your bedroom mess included. Then challenge yourself to vacuum the whole house in high speed. This will rev up your bod and shock your mom at the same time! Then, at every commercial, do five modified push-ups and ten ab crunches! Since there are typically eight commercials per half hour, that would be forty push-ups and eighty crunches. Who knew?

Get some spiritual conditioning every day at www.youthwalk.org. or www.briomag.com/brio magazine/spiritualhealth.

fession!) Or believe the promise that when you obey your parents, life will go well for you (see Ephesians 6:1–3). Who doesn't want that? Or trust Jesus when he says he is always with you—knowing you have a forever friend can change your life! So firming up your faith leads to a more confident, assured you! It allows you to be a B.A.B.E. who now feels her best and is ready to *be* her best.

Circuit training is performing preplanned exercises, going from one to another without resting in between until you've completed all the exercises in the "circuit." The big bonus with circuit training is that it increases cardiopulmonary fitness (yep, that's your heart and lungs) while toning muscles and increasing overall body strength. Plus, this routine combines both whole body (aerobic) and selected muscle group (targeted) exercises, ranging from low to high intensity, which is exactly what your body needs. It's a total-body workout.

Want to try it? Go to www.andreastephens .com, find Hot Topics: Health and Fitness, then select "Mix It Up with a Circuit Workout." This fast-paced routine is pure fitness fun.

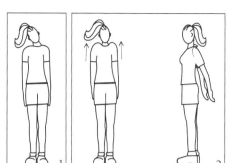

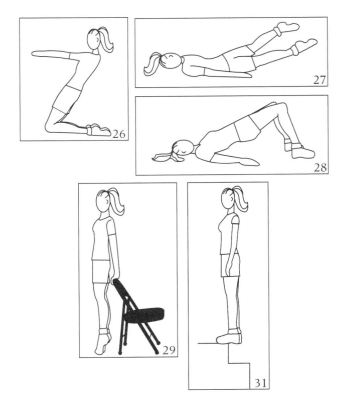

10

GRACEFUL GIRL

"Me, graceful?" Could be! What does the word *graceful* mean to you? You may think of flowing dancers, pageant contestants, figure skaters, or even a performance on the uneven bars. *Graceful* means ease of movement—smooth, flowing, unforced gestures that come naturally. They may come naturally because of inborn coordination, or because someone has been taught correct movements and has practiced them to the point that they look natural and very graceful.

Developing a Graceful Manner

Have you ever noticed, though, that not everyone appears graceful in the same situations? You may feel graceful cruising on your bike but totally awkward in aerobic dance class. Maybe you have a friend who's an awesome pitcher with a natural unforced throw. But put her in a pair of heels on prom night and watch a disaster unfold! This is due to our individual, God-given body types or frames, as Psalm 139:13, 15 describes:

For You formed my inward parts. . . . My frame was not hidden from You, when I was made in secret.

NASB

Every B.A.B.E. is graceful in her own way. When you're taking a look at your own gracefulness, be fair. Don't judge it by someone else's standards. You are you. Discover the areas where being graceful comes naturally, and in situations where you feel less than comfortable, work on it! Why? Because even if you think this graceful talk is too prissy for you, there will be a time when you have to stand in front of a group to give a speech or want to apply for your dream job. Do you want to let crummy posture or a sloppy appearance get in the way? I didn't think so.

Of course, gracefulness can be developed through knowing what moves appear graceful, and through practice. Yes, *practice*. And self-discipline! It's almost like homework—you have to apply what you're learning before it makes any sense. So apply what you're going to learn—right here and right now—about developing a graceful manner, also known as visual poise.

God-Confidence

One reason I love teaching poise principles is because, over and over, it has proven to boost a B.A.B.E.'s confidence level. Knowing that in a given situation you *look* your best, you will also *feel* your best, and that helps you *be* your best.

Every one of us has reasons to stand up straight, hold our head up, look others in the eye, and feel confident about who we are. Can you think of some reasons? How about these:

You are special and unique—one of a kind.
You are valuable and loved by God.
You are fully female—a prize creation totally worth
    celebrating.

You are alive! You are a human life, and *every* life has value.

Perhaps you have achievements and accomplishments associated with your name—academics, sports, animals, arts, crafts, church, or community work.

As a Christian, you are a child of God, and the Holy Spirit lives in you.

You have special abilities. Plus, God has put spiritual gifts and talents inside you to be used for him.

Add your own personal stats here:

Even more important than this list is the fact that you have God-confidence—or at least you can! Why would I make such a strong statement? First of all, if you have put your faith and trust in Jesus Christ as your personal Lord and Savior, you are a child of God! His Holy Spirit lives inside you. You are never on your own. You never have to do anything alone. You have power-packed potential that is Spirit driven.

Second, as a B.A.B.E. you have come to understand that you are **beautiful** in God's eyes—a one-of-a-kind masterpiece with a beauty all your own. You don't have to strive to match up to some unattainable beauty or sexy image. You are fully **accepted** by him, and since you have made him your "audience of One," you no longer live to please and impress everyone else! You are free to be yourself and bask in your Maker's unconditional love. Plus, God has **blessed** you with spiritual blessings—things that he has freely given and no one can take away! Your special abilities (academic, athletic, artistic) and spiritual gifts (service, hospitality, encouragement, faith) were hand-selected by your heavenly Father. Finally, you have been created with a specific purpose in mind, something that God will show you as you stay tight with him, something that will make a difference in your life and in the lives of others, something that is **eternally significant**.

As a B.A.B.E., you are here *on* purpose and *for* a purpose! And it's all a God-thing.

That is **God-confidence**! You aren't hung up on what you can or can't do (or be) in your *own* strength. You are focused on what *God* is all about and therefore what *you* are all about *because* of him.

The Bible says in Proverbs 3:26 that the Lord is your confidence. He is the foundation and the purpose for your confidence. Your other achievements, talents, gifts, and relationships are just added bonuses. You can believe in the person God has made *you* by putting your confidence in him.

Hebrews 10:35 instructs us not to throw away confidence in ourselves or in God, because it has great rewards, especially since it is built on the solid, unchanging foundation of God's Word.

Are you feeling more confident now? Do you see how to develop and increase real confidence? Now that we know how to develop it, let's show it in our visual poise.

Glam Tip: Show your confidence in your handshake. When you meet someone for the first time (or when you're initially seeing them out somewhere), extend your hand, offering a friendly shake. Place the backward "L" (made by your thumb and index finger) into the "L" on their hand. Wrap your fingers around their hand, giving a gentle squeeze. Do *not* do the limp-hand thing. It says, "Hey, I'm *not* into touching you or getting to know you. I'm sort of insecure and not sure if you will like me." Forget that! Even if you do feel a bit unsure, shake hands like a confident B.A.B.E.!

What Is Visual Poise?

Let's define *visual poise*. *Visual* means what can be seen with the eyes, or the outward appearance. *Poise* is your composure or the way you carry yourself—the way you control your body movements. Therefore, *visual poise* is your outward control of your body movements, as seen by others. Sounds technical, doesn't it?

But don't worry. What you are going to learn will help you relax. You won't have to be preoccupied with yourself, wondering whether or not you look good. Knowing that you look your best will give you the freedom to get your attention off yourself. This is real B.A.B.E.-ness at its best—being as *un*self-conscious as possible and therefore focused on others!

In the beginning of the how-tos of visual poise, we need to start at the very core of what will be the foundation of your newly acquired gracefulness—your posture.

What Difference Does Posture Make?

Posture is best defined as the positioning of your body structure or, more simply, body alignment. Your posture is very important. Whether or not you realize it, your posture sends messages to others about who you are and how you feel about yourself. Your posture talks! It is part of other people's first impression of you.

What impression do you want to give others through your posture? What does *your* body positioning tell others about you? Are you confident, insecure, or arrogant? Friendly, withdrawn, or unapproachable? Sloppy, shy, or snobbish? Nice, rebellious, or just whatever? Is your posture telling the truth about you?

As a teen, I personally learned to develop the posture that says, "I like myself, and I know who I am as God's child. Now I want to know *you*." You can develop your posture too.

Good Posture Pointers

1. Keeping your chin parallel with the floor, hold your head directly above your shoulders. Don't thrust your neck forward or pull it backward.

2. Pull your shoulders slightly back, if needed. This does not mean shoulders go upward to the ears! Back means *back*.

3. Lift your rib cage. Put your hand at the base of your ribs, then take a deep breath. Feel your rib cage lift? Hold it there, using the lower rib area to breathe. *Don't* take a deep breath and hold it. Your ribs and lungs are not connected. You can lift your rib cage and breathe normally at the same time. Also, it's nearly impossible for your shoulders to slump forward if your rib cage is lifted properly.

4. If you have a tendency to stand with your lower back arched, gently rotate your pelvis area forward. Don't exaggerate! This is a good time to tighten your abdominal muscles.

5. Let your arms hang naturally at your sides. When walking, slightly swing your arms. This should be a controlled movement. No floppy arms allowed! Your arm swing will naturally be in proportion to your step length. For example, when you're in a hurry and your steps are longer, your arm swing increases just a bit.

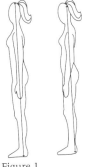

6. Check yourself from a side view. Good body alignment looks like figure 1. If someone drew a straight line down your body, would it run through the center of your ear, neck, shoulder, elbow, hip, knee, and ankle? Adjust your body alignment where it's needed.

7. Now the icing on the cake: your facial expression! Good posture can be totally trashed by a nasty expression. What is your face revealing to others? Take a good look. Even go so far as to practice pleasant expressions in front of a mirror so you can memorize how they feel. Happy smiling!

Figure 1.
Good vs. poor posture.

The Posture Workout

Like all your muscles, your "posture muscles" (delts, lats, abs) need regular exercise to become toned. If you are finding some of the posture points a challenge, try these exercises for quicker and better results.

Positive Results of Correct Alignment and Posture

You have more vocal power because your diaphragm is not squished.
Your inner organs have plenty of room to function.
You can look more slender through your waistline.
Your clothes will fit better.
You can help relieve stress on your body.
You will feel better about yourself.

Shoulder blade builders. Using both hands, take a heavy can or a three-pound dumbbell and lift it directly over your head. Bending your elbows, slowly lower the can behind your head, down toward the middle of your shoulder blades. Hold for thirty seconds, then slowly raise the can to the starting position. Repeat five to ten times. (Your triceps love this one.)

Next, lift your arms out to your sides, then move them backwards as far as you're able to reach. Hold fifteen seconds; relax. Repeat the exercise ten times.

Lower back boosters. Lean your back against a wall with your feet shoulder-width apart and fourteen inches away from the baseboard. Slowly slide down the wall to a sitting position—like on an invisible chair. Press the small of your back against the wall. Hold as long as possible, then slide back up the wall, returning to the starting position. Repeat five to ten times. (Your abs and quads are awake now!)

Next, lie with your back flat on the floor, your hands extended above your head, knees up, feet flat on the floor. Press your abdominals down toward the floor (think belly to spine) so that the small of your back presses against it. Hold ten seconds. Repeat ten times.

Swayback switcher. Lean your back against a wall with your feet shoulder-width apart and ten inches away from the baseboard. Bend forward all the way to the floor, keeping your hips against the wall and your knees slightly flexed. Slowly, pressing one vertebra at a time against the wall, lift to an upright position. Your head should be the last part of your body to touch the wall. Repeat five to ten times.

Balance booster. Standing straight and tall, bend your right knee, slowly raising your leg about twelve inches off the floor. Count to ten, lower your leg. Repeat with left leg. Repeat the exercise again, but this time bend and straighten your knee ten times on each leg. A balancing B.A.B.E.!

Sticky Shoulders. Take a long piece of masking tape and attach one end to the front part of your left shoulder (over bare skin, then put a shirt on). Pull your shoulders back into the correct position. Bring

---

Q: "I've noticed that when I'm on the computer or at school carrying my backpack, I pull my neck forward. Is that bad?"

A: Yes! Not only do you jut your chin forward while you're surfing the Web, but due to the weight of your backpack, you're leaning forward and leading with your head in order to compensate for those books you're lugging around! It's hard to walk or stand straight with a heavy backpack. So pay attention to your posture at all times to avoid headaches, muscle strain, disc herniations, pinched nerves, or early onset of arthritis.

Extra tips:
• Every half hour, sit up straight, then pull your neck and head straight back. Hold for a count of three, then release. Do ten reps.
• When sitting, place a small pillow behind your lower back. This extra support will bring your shoulders back.
• Think of walking with your rib cage lifted—like someone was pulling a string upward from the center of your chest. It's almost impossible to jut your chin out if your rib cage is properly lifted.
• Don't wear your backpack over one shoulder. Distribute the weight evenly. Try to minimize the weight of the pack. Yeah, this might mean leaving a few personal items at home, but your neck will thank you for it!
• Try raising your computer monitor so that the top half of the screen is at eye level.
• Stick this note on your computer screen: "Sit straight, lift head!"
• Buddy up with a friend who will help you remember your new posture!

the masking tape back around the shoulder, all the way across your back, and attach the other end to the front of your right shoulder. Every time your shoulders want to slump forward, they will pull on the tape. What a great reminder!

Take a Stance

You might be saying, "Now that I'm holding my body right, what do I do with my feet?" Great question. There are two ways to stand that will give you a poised and confident appearance. The key ingredient in both of these positions is this: keep your knees and ankles close together!

Side-by-side stance. Put your feet together, pointing them straight forward with your knees touching, if possible, and slightly flexed, not locked. Keep your weight equally distributed on both feet—leaning on one leg or cocking out a hip looks sloppy and throws off body alignment.

Model's stance. In this stance, only your front foot faces directly forward, while your back foot is at a 45 degree angle. Touch the heel of your front foot to the arch (or center) area of your back foot. Put your weight on your back foot, allowing your front knee to be relaxed.

Now, where can you put these two stances to use? How about:

In front of a group

Waiting in line (like the school lunch line or the theater)

At a fancy occasion

ANDREA'S ADVICE

Slightly turning your hips, putting your body at about a three-quarter angle, gives them a more graceful look. Plus, placing your weight on your back foot will allow you to take your first step using your front foot. That's how it's done in the modeling world!

Unless you take an expensive modeling course, who'd ever teach you these great secrets to being a graceful girl? Me!

At an interview

When having your picture taken

In a fashion show

Anytime

The Feminine Stride

I know, you learned to walk years ago. But I have a few hints to share that may improve the style of your walk. Everyone knows that as glamour girls, we are to walk with one foot *directly* in front of the other. But do you know why? (Other than the fact that we'd be walking sideways if we didn't?) Try this simple test.

Stand with your feet about ten inches apart. Draw an imaginary line across your hips, down one leg, across the feet, and up the other leg, back to where you started. What shape did you just create? A rectangle. Now try this: place your left foot directly in front of your right as if you were taking a step. Draw another line across your hips, down one leg to your feet and up the other leg. The shape? A triangle, or a V shape. Considering both shapes, which one is more feminine? I hope you said the V shape. Walking with one foot directly in front of the other looks feminine and graceful because of the shape.

Toed-out toes? As you walk, you may notice something about your feet. When you take a step, your foot is slightly "toed out." In other words, the position of your foot is at a *slight* angle. This is for balance and is normal. If you were to walk a straight line, the inner edge of your heel and the edge of your big toe knuckle would be just touching the line. Notice the line is not running through the middle of the big toe.

Maintain great balance by keeping your weight evenly distributed as

Q: "How can I know if my steps are too big?"

A: The average length of a step is usually one and a half times your foot length. Of course, your step length will vary depending on how fast you walk. If you are dragging your heels while walking (this will detract from your walking style and wear the heels off your shoes very quickly), then chances are your steps are too big.

you walk. Slightly flex your knees—don't lock them with each step. You're after a smooth, gliding look to your walk, not a bounce.

Control those hips! With your hips facing forward, bring each leg through the hip joint smoothly, making sure you don't throw it sideways with each step. Doing this will keep you from looking floppy or flirty and may help you avoid future back problems.

Walk upright, girl! Avoid leaning into your walk. In fact, no part of your body needs to take the lead! Remember, keep your rib cage lifted, chin parallel to the floor, arms swinging naturally, palms facing your outer thighs.

Turning with Purpose

I've seen girls get their feet and legs twisted up and even trip over their own feet when they attempt to turn around. Let's not let that happen to you! If you know *how* you're going to turn, it will be smooth sailing.

Start by planning ahead and choosing the spot where you're going to turn. Just like in ballet or gymnastics, this is called "spotting." Then, instead of making your next step a full-size step, place the heel of one foot directly in front of the toes of your other foot. There will be only an inch or so of space between your feet. Next, slightly lift up on the balls of your feet and turn halfway around so that you're facing the opposite direction. Did your legs get twisted? Think this through. When you begin the turn, if your right foot is forward, you'll turn to the left. Likewise, if your left foot is forward, you'll turn to the right.

Did you notice that, after you turned, your back foot became your front foot and your front foot became your back? Be sure your back foot ends up in a 45 degree angle, as it is in the model's stance. In fact, you should be in the model's stance when you end the turn (with your weight on your back foot). Remember, practice makes perfect—or *close* to perfect anyway.

"Walk in a manner worthy of the calling with which you have been called" (Ephesians 4:1 NASB).

Walking with Whom?

Have you ever heard anyone ask, "How is your walk with the Lord?" What does that mean? Here the term *walk* refers to a day-to-day journey or a relationship. "How is your relationship with the Lord?" is what the person is really asking.

You are in a special relationship with God, on a continuous journey through life with the One who loves you the most. This relationship, unlike others, will last forever. Jesus has promised that he will never leave you or turn away from you. The Lord is here to be your best friend. Are you spending time with him daily, talking over every problem facing you, sharing your joys and disappointments?

Just as we would do if we wanted to get to know someone new at school, we must spend time getting to know God. It's time well spent. Talk to him. Read his Word. Your relationship or walk with the Lord is meant to be your best walk ever.

No Plopping Allowed

Sitting can be made less clumsy by applying a few simple techniques. As you approach a chair, spot where you would turn around in order to sit down, then actually turn. Hopefully you'll end up very close to the front edge of the chair. Back up until you can feel your calf touching the edge of the chair. You know the chair is there

because you can feel it. You don't have to look over your shoulder at the chair or turn to touch it to be sure it's behind you. We've all probably experienced the embarrassment of falling flat on our behinds because someone pulled a chair out from under us. Ouch! But when you're touching the chair with your calf, you can be sure you'll have a safe landing.

Using those power-packed quads (thigh muscles), slowly lower yourself straight down on the front part of the chair. No plopping down! Don't lean forward. Keep your back straight from the waist up. If you're sitting all the way to the back of the chair, then you went too far. Ideally, you want to be on the front third of the chair at this point.

Glam Tip: If you're wearing a skirt, pull the sides of it forward before you sit down. Do this right where your hands hang to your sides. Don't tuck your skirt under your buttocks when you are in the process of sitting—it will only draw attention to where you don't want it.

Next, place your palms, with your fingers closed, on the tops of your upper thighs. Gently lift your body, pressing your hands to your thighs as resistance, and move to the back of the chair. Adjust yourself so you're comfortable.

Hands and Feet

Okay, now you're sitting, so what do you do with the rest of you? Try some of these suggestions for your hands:

Place your hands together, one on top of the other, with both palms down.

Place your hands together with the bottom hand palm up and the top hand palm down on top of the other hand.

Loosely interlock fingers from both hands, creating a V shape (not a fist).

Avoid crossing your arms, playing with your hair, or fussing with your clothes.

Now for your feet. Try any of these positions for a very together look. (Key: knees together, ankles together.)

Line up both feet directly under your knees, feet together.

Place both feet off to one side, ankles close together.

Cross your feet at the ankles. Position your feet off to one side so your knees won't fall open.

Crossing your legs with one knee right on top of the other can be tough on circulation (though it's fun to swing your leg). But since you'll cross them anyway, at least try this technique that eases up on the circulation dilemma and gives a slenderizing look. As you cross your legs, go beyond your knees, putting one leg on top of the other. In other words, if possible, cross your legs above the knees. Pull them to one side.

Avoid twisting your feet around the leg of the chair.

Avoid sitting with one foot sideways on top of your other knee, the way many guys do!

When you're ready to get up out of the chair, uncross your legs or ankles and place them directly beneath your knees. If they're too far under the chair you'll have a hard time getting up. You might even want to try placing one foot a little bit ahead of the other. Place your palms on top of your thighs, using them as resistance to push yourself up. Try lifting with your back straight, rather than diving forward in order to get momentum to lift out of the chair.

These sitting secrets may take an extra bit of practice, but you'll be glad you took the time to perfect them.

Managing Stairs One Step at a Time

Just a word on going up and down stairs. Using your correct posture, try to glide rather than bounce up and down the steps. Do this by keeping your knees flexed every time you take a step. Locking your knees causes a jerk in your movement. Keep your knees slightly bent. To help you get the feel of not locking your knees with each step, practice walking around with both of your knees slightly bent. Feel the control in your thighs? The thighs are where true control for a smooth glide up or down the stairs really is.

When you're moving up the stairs, your heel touches the step first, then your toes. Use your toes

ANDREA'S ADVICE

Put these graceful girl tips to work when you interview for a job you really want. Get excellent interview instructions from my book *Stuff a Girl's Gotta Know.*

to lift you up to the next step. Reach with your toes to the lower step when moving down the stairs. Be sure you place your entire foot on the step.

You may want to try walking on the stairs at a slight angle. This is not as difficult as it may sound. Keep your upper body fairly straight while you turn your lower body at a slight angle. It doesn't matter whether you turn to the right or left. Concentrate on looking downward at the steps with your *eyes only*, not with your entire head. Walking the stairs at an angle adds a touch of dignity and style to your appearance.

Are you on your way to becoming a gracious woman? Sure, it won't happen overnight, but it's not impossible! When you're practicing your outer visual poise technique, don't forget to practice your inner poise. A gracious woman is precious in the sight of God and others.

ANDREA'S ADVICE

Complement your outer poise with inner poise! When I think of the women I've known who are poised inwardly, the word that comes to my mind is *gracious*. A gracious woman is one who is very grateful for all she has. She is rarely greedy or jealous over the belongings of others. She is content. She has a quiet and gentle spirit about her. She is a good listener and doesn't get angry very easily. She is kind, courteous, and graceful, and she does things in good taste. She is merciful and shows compassion to others. Not only does she have outward control, but she also has inward control.

Want more? Want to know the best ways to handle your purse, put on a jacket, yawn discreetly, or shake hands? It's all at www.andrea stephens.com under Hot Topics: Body Image.

11

BREATHTAKING BEAUTY

When I was in high school, I was totally obsessed with beauty. I stared at magazine covers, gorgeous makeup ads, and fashion layouts all the time. People whom our culture had stamped as beautiful really had it all together—right? They had an upper hand on life—right? They got preferred treatment because they were special—right? That's what I thought. I was wrong.

It was when I was modeling in New York that God opened my eyes to see the real definition of the word *beauty*. Actually, the whole lesson centered on Janice (not her real name). Here's what happened.

The test board at Wilhelmina consisted of the new models. We were the ones who were green to the business. We spent most of our time taking test pictures, hoping to put together a dynamic portfolio. That's when I met Janice. She was one of those girls with thick and bouncy hair, straight white teeth, clear skin, tiny hips, and an upper body that just couldn't be missed.

One afternoon after a photo shoot, I stopped in at the agency. The room buzzed with ringing telephones, busy bookers, and a few models, including Janice. The attention, as usual, centered on her. Everyone seemed to be in awe of Janice's sudden weight loss. I listened to her exaggerated explanation of how "it was nothing." She had just taken up jogging and started eating less. "After all," she exclaimed, "what is there worth eating anyway?"

Are you kidding? I thought. If New York doesn't add to one's fat layer, nothing will. Every corner has a vendor selling some sort of tempting treat. Trail mix, roasted cashews, hot dogs, and pizza by the slice! I was pudging out underneath my oversized sweater, but not Janice. She had taken up jogging. I had tried jogging too: I jogged two blocks up to the Bagel Nosh, got two cinnamon-raisin bagels to go, and jogged back. Obviously, Janice and I were not using the same method of jogging!

As I sat there listening, the subject changed to Janice's new boy-friend, how hot his body was, and all their partying adventures. Janice's language turned crude, and I began to feel uncomfortable. The longer I looked and listened, the more unattractive she became. Her physical beauty began to crumble before my eyes as the "yuck" poured out of her mouth.

Eventually Janice strutted off to her next appointment. That's when I discovered the truth about her weight loss. "Want to know what I heard about Janice's 'Oh, it was nothing' weight loss?" one of the models asked in a daring tone of voice. "Janice didn't sweat one drop to lose a pound. She just popped pills." She paused. "Speed." A hush came over the room. *Drugs?* And I had thought she had it all. Janice looked great on the outside, but between the comments about her boy toy and this drug thing, there was very little real beauty.

I learned a lesson that day: who you are on the inside is far more important than what you look like on the outside. Outside beauty alone is like having an elegant, hand-cut crystal vase with no flowers in it. Real beauty is more than being able to offer the world a frosty smile on the cover of a magazine. It's more than starring in a flick or being a skinny chick. It means being a person who is honest and cares for others—a person who can laugh and cry with others.

Beauty Bonus with Rachel Wightman, Brio Girl 2006:
Beauty does not rely on the clothes you wear, how much makeup is caked on your face, or how many guys have your phone number. True beauty comes from within. When someone has a beautiful heart and a beautiful spirit, it shines through and she glows with the love of Christ. Beauty cannot be defined; it is displayed.

What Is Real Beauty?

When I ask girls to define real beauty, many tell me they think of someone who is kind, unselfish, and loving toward others. You might say a person with real beauty is one who shares her happy attitude, one who is patient in trying situations, one who is kind and inclusive to girls at school—even to the ones no one else likes. Each of these describes loving and thoughtful *actions* rather than appearance.

Think about the important people in your life. Are they special because of what they look like? No, it's probably because of their kindness, loyalty, and friendship, or maybe because they're always there when you need them.

Jesus was like that. People didn't like him because he was tall, dark, and handsome. It was because of the person he was on the inside. Isaiah 53:2 tells us, "He [Jesus] has no form or comeliness [royal, kingly pomp], that we should look at Him, and no beauty that we should desire Him" (AMP).

You mean that Jesus wasn't the suave, macho type like the guys you daydream about? No. What was it, then, that caused people to be drawn to him by the thousands? What made Jesus so magnetic? Real beauty!

Jesus was kind to the woman at the well. He traveled miles to lay hands on people who were sick. He came along at the right moment to assist fishermen with their catch for the day. He made time in his busy schedule for those who needed his forgiveness. He served others by providing food for them and by washing the disciples' feet. He gave of himself to show that he cared. Ultimately he gave everything: he gave his life for us.

It wasn't Jesus's appearance that made him beautiful. It was his heart.

It works the same for you and me as B.A.B.E.s. What's in your heart will affect the amount of real beauty you have. Usually what's in your heart determines what your actions will be.

It's true that we notice the outer appearance of others first. Then we get to know them and we can see who they really are, what they're all about. That's where God looks first. He wants us to be beautiful inside and to be like him; after all, we are created in his image. He wants us to have the same three "c" characteristics that he has—compassion, contentment, and consistency. These are three key building blocks to real beauty. Let's take a look.

Building Blocks to Real Beauty

Compassion

Katie had worked earnestly in anticipation of this day. Fancy footsteps, routines, high kicks, enthusiastic smiles—she had mastered them all in hopes of winning the judges' favor. Cheerleading tryouts were today.

When Katie arrived early at the gym where the tryouts were to be held, she drew a number from the big fishbowl to see where she would fall in tryout order. Number two. She was thrilled. This would give her a chance to perform for the judges before almost all of the other girls. It meant everything to Katie to make it as a cheerleader, and being number two was more than she could have asked for.

The other girls arrived. Some were excited, some scared. All were frantically practicing cheers under their breath.

"God sees not as man sees, for man looks at the outward appearance, but the LORD looks at the heart" (1 Samuel 16:7 NASB).

Katie looked at her watch. Only a few more minutes, and her big moment would be here.

Anxiously looking around, Katie noticed Jenna, a friend from English class, standing away from the others. Jenna looked rather distressed. Surely something wasn't right. Katie was concerned, so she made her way through swinging arms and kicking legs over to Jenna.

"Hey, Jenna," Katie greeted her.

"Oh, hi, Katie," Jenna responded quickly, without looking up.

"Everyone is so excited about tryouts. They're practicing like crazy. Did you want to practice? I mean, if you need help with a cheer, I could help you real quick." Katie rushed the words out, knowing tryouts were about to start.

"No thanks, Katie. I know the cheers pretty well. That's not the problem." Jenna lifted her eyes to look at Katie. "I just found out that my grandpa was rushed to the hospital, and I want to get over there, but I've worked so hard for the tryouts. I've always wanted to be a cheerleader. And can you believe it—I'm number twenty-seven out of twenty-nine girls trying out." Jenna's gaze dropped. "I don't know if I can wait that long."

Katie instantly felt a pang in her stomach. She cared about Jenna and knew how awful she must feel. But if she traded her number she might ruin her chances at making the cheerleading squad. *Well,* she thought, *if I make it, I make it. If I don't, I don't.* Jenna's grandfather was more important than wanting to perform first.

"Listen, Jenna, I drew number two. Why don't we trade numbers? Then you can get over to the hospital and be with your grandpa."

"Seriously?" Jenna asked in a hopeful voice.

"Yeah, for real." Katie smiled.

"Number two," the squad director shouted from the other end of the gym. Katie traded her number with Jenna's. After a quick hug, Jenna darted toward the tryout room. Just to see her so excited was worth the trade-off to Katie.

Describe a person you know who has real beauty. What does she act like, look like, and do for others?

Katie took notice of her friend's feelings and needs. But she did more than notice, she did something about it! That's true compassion! Some people are too wrapped up in their own lives to even notice that someone else is hurting or in need. But compassion drives those with real beauty. They go ahead and help when it's needed, hug when it comforts, and often do the odd little jobs no one else wants to do.

Compassionate people are not selfish. They're willing to put others before themselves. They're kind, loving, and willing to get involved in others' lives. Being compassionate toward others is a quality that enhances relationships and develops real beauty.

Are you aware of the feelings and needs of those closest to you? List the names of your family members. Next to their names jot down what you think their needs are. How can you help fulfill those needs?

Glam Tip: You're writing a paper, cramming for an exam, running late for a rehearsal, or whatever, when you are interrupted in a very untimely fashion. When you respond to the person (be it your mom or little sister) with a patient smile and gentle words, your true beauty will be showing!

Contentment

Contentment is a characteristic found in girls with real beauty. Being content means being thankful and glad for who you are and what you have. Content people have learned to gracefully accept life's ups and downs, choosing to make the best of every situation. How? By trusting God with their lives and situations, and trusting that if the God who loves them more than anyone else knows what they need, he'll give it to them.

Being content on the inside brings you a true sense of joy and peace. Smiles come easily. Encouraging others seems natural. You are into loving life!

Your life becomes about focusing your attention on others

ANDREA'S ADVICE

Be graciously willing to accept what God has given you. Be grateful to him for loving you and providing for your needs. Then you will have a heart that is content and full!

rather than worrying about yourself. God's got your back and you know it!

Do you know people who are content? Aren't they peaceful and calming to be around? They really help us keep our focus on the things that matter, especially the Lord. People with real beauty are people others want to spend their time with. And one of the reasons is that they have learned to be content.

Contentment is a real-beauty quality. It leads to an attitude of gratitude, not grumpitude (okay, I made up that word). How do you currently rate on the contentment scale?

Consider these questions, then rate yourself. On a scale of 0 to 10, 0 is very discontented and 10 is very contented.

CONTENTMENT QUIZ
Are You Gracious or Grumpcious?

1. Do you feel peaceful about the way your life is going?

   0   1   2   3   4   5   6   7   8   9   10

2. Does your stomach turn every time you see someone who just got their license show up in a brand-new car?

   0   1   2   3   4   5   6   7   8   9   10

3. Do you wish you could get your hair to look the way someone else's does?

   0   1   2   3   4   5   6   7   8   9   10

4. Are you satisfied with the special body God has given you?

   0   1   2   3   4   5   6   7   8   9   10

5. Do you feel anxious about going to a guy's sixteenth birthday party, especially since you couldn't afford a new outfit?

   0   1   2   3   4   5   6   7   8   9   10

6. Would you be excited to hear you were going to Grandma's again on vacation, or would you feel cheated that you weren't headed to Disney World or the Bahamas?

   0   1   2   3   4   5   6   7   8   9   10

7. Have you ever avoided bringing your friends to your house because of where it was and what it looked like?

   0   1   2   3   4   5   6   7   8   9   10

8. Do you get seriously bummed out when you don't get the privileges other teens do, like late curfew, class trips, or private telephone lines?

0   1   2   3   4   5   6   7   8   9   10

So in general, are you content? Do you see room for improvement? Need to banish grumpitude and expand your gratitude? Be glad for what God has given you, no matter how much or how little!

Consistency

Consistency is one of those words with a heavy-duty meaning. Karen found that out the hard way. She used to always shop, go for ice cream, and hang out with Jamie. They had even gone on a mission trip together. But recently Karen just kept breaking plans or telling Jamie she was too busy. She even leaked a secret about Jamie that she'd promised to keep. Rather than being honest like a

---

Q: "What's the big deal about Christians having joy?"

A: When joy is bubbling deep within you, it stirs up and produces some terrific stuff!

First of all, joy makes you feel better. Get this! The Bible says a merry, cheerful, joyful heart acts like a medicine to our bodies (see Proverbs 17:22). Joy and laughter bring healing to our physical ailments. Science has backed this up. It's been proven that a certain chemical is released into our bloodstream when we laugh or have a joyful attitude. This chemical triggers health! It strengthens the immune system. A joyful person is less likely to become sick in the first place. Not only does her joy keep her out of the doctor's office, it helps others! Joy spreads! If you are joyful, you can't help but splash some onto someone else!

Second, joy—in the Lord—gives us strength (see Nehemiah 8:10). Joy gives us mental, emotional, and physical strength (of course, not the same physical strength that comes from pumping up your muscles at the gym).

The psalmist instructs us to delight ourselves in the Lord (see Psalm 37:4). That means to find joy in him.

good friend, she made up excuses for ditching Jamie and hanging with other girls.

Jamie felt confused. She and Karen had been friends for years. They could always count on each other. When they spent time together, they talked about everything. Because Karen had become wishy-washy, Jamie felt hurt. She wasn't sure anymore if Karen was such a good friend. When they were together, Jamie felt reluctant to share things with Karen. She had lost trust in her. It was difficult to confide in someone who was a friend one minute but not the next. Eventually Jamie stopped calling Karen and made new friends.

Karen had really lost out. She valued Jamie's friendship but wasn't committed enough to be there when Jamie called. Karen had not been consistent in her actions and friendship with Jamie.

Consistency may be the hardest to develop of the three qualities. Being wishy-washy, moody, uncommitted, and unpredictable are the opposites of being consistent. The "yo-yo" person who is up and down, yes and no, or maybe so will have a harder time building trust and respect in friendships with others. People who are consistent are people you can count on. They're people who are confident in being themselves—no masks, no games.

Consistency takes practice. We don't always feel like acting the same or following through on what we say we will do. That's why being consistent is a decision you make, not a feeling.

On a separate sheet of paper, write a brief description of a friend who is consistent and another who is inconsistent. Which one can you count on? Which category would you fit into?

Jesus is consistent. He isn't loving one minute, mean the next. He doesn't act like a friend to your face and then talk behind your back. He doesn't act concerned with your troubles and then blow you off. He is consistent. That's one reason we can trust him.

Read about Jesus's consistency in Hebrews 13:8. How does knowing this affect your relationship with Jesus?

Like compassion and contentment, consistency can be learned. We can decide to embrace all three of these real-beauty qualities and follow through on them with our actions. However, this whole process is much easier with the help of the Holy Spirit. The Holy Spirit oversees the construction process going on inside of you and me, and he builds a more beautiful person on the inside.

Under Construction

Ever wonder, "Why do I always feel I'm under construction? Will I ever have *real* beauty that shines from the inside out?" It may seem like you grow in one area, then the Lord shines his spotlight on another, and the inner-beauty construction process begins all over again. It's a journey. You're continuously under construction. The Holy Spirit works with you to build beauty from the inside out. People who are filled with beauty on the inside radiate beauty on the outside, no matter what they look like physically.

I encourage you never to give up during the construction process. There are times you will want to toss in the towel—but don't. Holly didn't. Hanging in there sure paid off for her.

Holly heard about Jesus at camp and gave her heart and life to him soon after. The decision to follow Christ seemed easy enough at the time, but now she was finding it shaky to be sixteen and to live for Jesus. She felt so discouraged she just wanted to quit. "Why does it matter what I act like and what I do?" she wanted to know.

Holly's Bible study group met for breakfast before school on Wednesday mornings. They were in the middle of a study on the fruit of the Spirit when Holly started questioning herself. *Love, joy, peace, patience . . .* Patience was the one that stumped her. She was having a hard time learning to be patient. Where was patience when she needed it the most, which was at home with her mom?

For the past couple of weeks, Holly's mom had really been getting on her nerves. She couldn't figure out why her

Q: "Does the Bible really change us?"

A: Hebrews 4:12 says, "The Word that God speaks is alive and full of power . . . exposing and sifting and analyzing and judging the very thoughts and purposes of the heart" (AMP). When we respond positively to God's Word and adjust ourselves to its teaching, then yes, it changes us!

mom was always telling her what to do. "Load the dishwasher, unload the dryer, clean your bedroom, dust the living room, finish your homework, babysit for the Stewarts so we can go to dinner with them, help your little brother with the trash." She never got a sufficient answer when she asked her mother, "But why?" "Because I said so," was not what she was looking for.

One night after a major explosion with her mother, Holly ran crying into her room. She slammed the door behind her. "Help me, Lord; I need more patience," she pleaded as she threw herself down on her bed. Holly really needed that patience she was learning about. Every time she spouted off to her mom, it made her feel ugly inside.

Holly could sense the Holy Spirit working to remind her to be patient. Suddenly the thoughts that came to her seemed to be just what she needed.

Holly knew from her Bible study that God wanted her to be patient. She needed to work *with* the Lord rather than *against* him. She needed to decide to act patient in the situations with her mom. It made sense to her. Holly thought back to the fight she'd just had with her mother. If only she had chosen to be patient, as the Holy Spirit was prompting her to do, instead of acting angry, as her feelings were telling her to do, the scene with her mom might have been totally different.

Holly's sense of discouragement began to lift. As the days went on she had plenty of opportunity to try out her theory. What a surprise—it worked! Patience grew in Holly. She didn't feel so ugly on the inside. She felt better about herself and her new behavior. Holly's patience on the inside was making her prettier on the outside. She could feel the construction under way, for with the Lord's help she could act patiently.

Like Holly, you are in process! How is the Holy Spirit working to build real beauty into your life?

Here are two Scriptures that are helpful during the real-beauty construction process: "The Lord will perfect that which concerns me" (Psalm 138:8 AMP). "For I am confident of this very thing, that He who began a good work in you will perfect it until the day of Christ Jesus" (Philippians 1:6 NASB).

Isn't that good news? God is doing good work in you and is perfecting all the things concerning you. And it never stops! The construction continues as you and the Lord work on building your inner self.

Beholding His Beauty

God's Word is his love letter to us. Reading that letter provides you with an opportunity to spend some very special time with Jesus. The more you know about him, the more time you will want to spend with him through reading and prayer. The more time you spend with Jesus, the more you become like him and the more his beauty fills you.

Psalm 27:4 makes this point clear: "One thing I have asked from the LORD, that I shall seek: That I may dwell in the house [presence] of the LORD all the days of my life, to behold the beauty of the LORD and to meditate in His temple" (NASB).

Q: "Does the Bible say that what we do is more important than what we look like?"

A: The woman described in Proverbs 31 was oozing with real beauty from the inside out! Let's see what is said about her: "Praise her for the many fine things she does. These good deeds of hers shall bring her honor and recognition from even the leaders of the nations" (Proverbs 31:31 TLB). Fine things and good deeds describe a woman who is a hard worker, a planner, and a responsible and dependable person. Yet never does it say anything about her physical appearance (other than she wears purple!). Real beauty is not seen in a mirror.

When you spend time in the Lord's presence and think about what it says in his Word, you, like Jesus, will shine with a beauty that comes from within—real beauty, lasting beauty. Second Corinthians 4:16 tells us that our outer appearance fades with age, but our inner self—our spirit, the real us—is made new and younger every day. Real beauty that comes from spending time with Jesus will last forever.

No amount of makeup, skin care, classy colors, or clothes can give you the confidence and inner beauty that Jesus can. All of his qualities are available to you because his spirit came to live inside you when you accepted Jesus into your heart. Developing real beauty is possible for all of us if we allow the Holy Spirit to play an active part in our lives.

God's Word is so important. Exactly what does "word" mean, and how can we get more of it into our day? Glad you asked.

The Bible uses two Greek words that English translates as "word." One is the Greek word *logos*. This is the "Word" John speaks about in John 1:1: "In the beginning was the Word" (NIV), referring to Christ. *Logos* is also used in verses where Jesus spoke healing for people, such as for the centurion's servant in Luke 7:7. Whenever Jesus was speaking about the "word" being fulfilled, he used the word *logos.*

The other word, *rhema*, talks about that which is spoken or written. That's the one we find in Ephesians 6 when Paul tells us that we need to be armed with "God's whole armor" that we "may be able successfully to stand up against [all] the strategies and the deceits of the devil" (verse 11 AMP). Verse 17 says, "And take the helmet of salvation and the sword that the Spirit wields, which is the Word [*rhema*] of God" (AMP).

God's Word—both Jesus as "the Word" and the words God spoke in the Bible—is the way to life eternal and to a fulfilled life on earth. As David says, it "is a lamp to my feet and a light to my path. I have sworn [an oath] and have confirmed it, that I will keep your righteous ordinances [hearing, receiving, loving, and obeying them]" (Psalm 119:105–6 AMP).

All of that means that we are to "lay up" God's Word "in our hearts" by reading and studying the Bible—regularly. I know, sometimes the Bible's hard to read, especially if you're still trying to tackle the Shakespearean language of the King James Version. But there are a lot of great translations of the Bible (like the New International Version, the New American Standard Bible, the New Living Translation, the Message Remix) that are far easier to read than your school textbooks.

You don't like to read, or you "really don't have time, with all the schoolwork" you have to do?

"Your word have I laid up in my heart, that I might not sin against You" (Psalm 119:11 AMP).

Beauty Bonus with Danielle Kimmey (Out of Eden): "I think the best thing you can do for your looks is to read God's Word. People can always tell by your face that you've been in the presence of God."

Did you know that you can get the Bible on cassette or CD? That way you can listen to it on your portable CD player (or download it on your iPod) while you're working out, jogging, or going from class to class. You can even get a "pillow" speaker, a little flat round thing that you plug into your player and put under your pillow before you go to sleep. In that happy time between drowsiness and deep sleep you can listen to the wonderful stories and teachings from the Bible. It's the best sleep aid you can find! Also, some people believe you can actually learn subliminally while you sleep.

Here's something else. When you sit down at your computer before school or when you get home, turn on Daily Encounter, a free daily devotion series that you can find on www.actsweb.org/subscribe.php. Devotions will get you focused on God's will for your life and help you develop those Christlike characteristics that make you a real beauty!

Use the chart on the next page as your personal Bible reading plan. When you complete a chapter in each book of the Bible, check it off. It will be fun to watch your progress. It will be cool to see the Bible changing you from the inside out. It will be rewarding to see yourself having real beauty. It will be a blast becoming a total B.A.B.E.!

The New Testament

Book	1	2	3	4	5	6	7	8	9	10	11	12	13	14	15	16	17	18	19	20	21	22	23	24	25	26	27	28
Matthew	1	2	3	4	5	6	7	8	9	10	11	12	13	14	15	16	17	18	19	20	21	22	23	24	25	26	27	28
Mark	1	2	3	4	5	6	7	8	9	10	11	12	13	14	15	16												
Luke	1	2	3	4	5	6	7	8	9	10	11	12	13	14	15	16	17	18	19	20	21	22	23	24				
John	1	2	3	4	5	6	7	8	9	10	11	12	13	14	15	16	17	18	19	20	21							
Acts	1	2	3	4	5	6	7	8	9	10	11	12	13	14	15	16	17	18	19	20	21	22	23	24	25	26	27	28
Romans	1	2	3	4	5	6	7	8	9	10	11	12	13	14	15	16												
1 Corinthians	1	2	3	4	5	6	7	8	9	10	11	12	13	14	15	16												
2 Corinthians	1	2	3	4	5	6	7	8	9	10	11	12	13															
Galatians	1	2	3	4	5	6																						
Ephesians	1	2	3	4	5	6																						
Philippians	1	2	3	4																								
Colossians	1	2	3	4																								
1 Thess.	1	2	3	4	5																							
2 Thess.	1	2	3																									
1 Timothy	1	2	3	4	5	6																						
2 Timothy	1	2	3	4																								
Titus	1	2	3																									
Philemon	1																											
Hebrews	1	2	3	4	5	6	7	8	9	10	11	12	13															
James	1	2	3	4	5																							
1 Peter	1	2	3	4	5																							
2 Peter	1	2	3																									
1 John	1	2	3	4	5																							
2 John	1																											
3 John	1																											
Jude	1																											
Revelation	1	2	3	4	5	6	7	8	9	10	11	12	13	14	15	16	17	18	19	20	21	22						

B.A.B.E. IN ACTION

Spread the Real Beauty Around!

In God's opinion, one of the most beautiful things you can do is share with others the news of his Son, Jesus. Yep! Take action and talk him up! To do that, you have to be prepared. He may ask you to do it in the morning, at noon, or at midnight! It may be in the school library, while you are at work, at the movies with friends, or in another country building a house for the poor.

He doesn't expect perfection, just obedience.

We are told to "go into all the world" and do what? Preach the gospel! Share the good news of Jesus's death, burial, and resurrection! Tell people that forgiveness and eternal life in heaven are available to them today. They can have a personal relationship with the living God who created them and loves them. Nonbelievers matter to God.

Sharing the gospel might be the most eternally significant assignment ever. And it's given to you, to me, to everyone who calls Jesus "Lord" and God "Father." "Always be prepared to give an answer to everyone who asks you to give the reason for the hope that you have. But do this with gentleness and respect" (1 Peter 3:15 NIV).

I don't want you to get caught not knowing what to say. That might make you feel guilty or ineffective. No need for that! Here's a simple ABC method you can use to get prepared.

A—Admit. Help your friends to see that they have a need for Jesus. They have messed up (and sinned). This is what keeps them

* Portions of this section are taken from *Stuff a Girl's Gotta Know* (Ann Arbor, MI: Vine Books, 2003), 101–2.

separated from God. They need to admit that they need Jesus to forgive them of their sins.

In a society like ours that teaches moral relativism, some teens think they haven't sinned—after all, if it feels good, do it—right? Wrong! The God of the universe (who created them) has standards for them. Just take the Ten Commandments. Ask them: Have you ever dishonored your parents? Ever lied? Ever stolen anything? Ever used God's name in vain? Ever wanted what belonged to someone else? If they say "yes" to even one of these questions, they have broken God's standard and have sinned.

B—Believe. Tell your friends about Jesus so they can believe he is God's Son, sent from heaven to die on the cross to pay the penalty for their sins. Remind them that the punishment for sin is death, but Jesus came to die in their place. After he died, God raised him back to life, and now Jesus offers your friends new life when they believe in him.

C—Confess (and commit). Now is the time your friends should confess their sins and commit their lives to Jesus. Explain that to receive his free gift of eternal life, they need only to pray and ask him into their hearts.

Encourage them to pray, in their own words, something like this:

Lord Jesus, thank you for loving me so much that you died on the cross for my sins. I realize my sin has separated me from God, so I ask you to forgive me of my sins so I will have eternal life and live forever in heaven with God. Jesus, I ask you into my heart and make you the Lord and Master of my life. Fill me with your Holy Spirit so I can live a life that honors you. In your name I pray. Amen.*

Get a detailed description of the gospel, including the Scriptures to back it up, at www .andreastephens.com (Hot Topics: God Stuff).

ABC! Easy to remember, right?

It's thought that about 80 percent of people come to Christ through a friend.

And about 86 percent of people accept Jesus into their lives before the age of eighteen. That means that *you* have the greatest chance of introducing your peers to Jesus *right now*! And when you do, be sure to celebrate! Throw a victory party! Scripture lets us in on a heavenly secret.

> There is rejoicing in the presence of the angels of God over one sinner who repents.
>
> Luke 15:10 NIV

Isn't God fun? He throws a party every time someone is born spiritually and becomes his child. Now, what should *you* do? Be a friend to the new Christian. Make sure she has a Bible. Pray with her. Invite her to church and youth group. Include her in a small group Bible study. Buy her a Christian CD.

Then do her the best favor ever! Explain to her that God created her and thinks she is **beautiful**. Tell her she doesn't have to do anything to make God like her—he **accepts** her and loves her with an unending love. Encourage her to identify the special abilities and spiritual gifts God has **blessed** her with. Help her seek after the **eternally significant** plans God has for her life. Show her she is a B.A.B.E., just like you!

That is really beautiful!

Becoming a B.A.B.E.

Everything about being a B.A.B.E. has to do with believing in God, having a personal relationship with his Son, Jesus Christ, by asking him to forgive your sin and come into your life and heart to be your saving Lord, and having his Holy Spirit actually living inside you. According to the Bible, that's when you become God's child, part of his forever family. As his child, you'll come to understand (by reading the Bible) that

>   you're **beautiful** in God's eyes
>   you're **accepted** unconditionally, without fear of rejection, by God
>   you're **blessed** with spiritual gifts and special abilities
>   you're **eternally significant** as you discover and live out the plan God has for your life

Beautiful, accepted, blessed, eternally significant! That makes you a B.A.B.E.!

It all starts with saying yes to God, yes to Jesus, yes to the Holy Spirit. If you've never done that, I invite you to pray a prayer something like this one:

Dear God,
I believe in you. I believe you created me and you love me. I believe you sent your Son, Jesus, to this earth to live a perfect life and then die on the cross for the sins of everyone—including me. Jesus, I ask you to forgive me for all the things I've done wrong. I invite you into my life to be my Savior and the Lord of my life. Please send your Holy

Spirit, right now, to come live inside me. Let my body be his home. Now, Father God, show me my beauty through your eyes, teach me about how you value and accept me, and help me keep my focus on you and you alone. Help me identify and develop the spiritual gifts the Holy Spirit has just given me, and show me how to use my life in a way that makes a difference, a way that is eternally significant. I want to shine for you! In Jesus's name I pray. Amen!

Congrats! You've just become an official B.A.B.E.!
Go tell someone!

You've been created *on* purpose and *for* a purpose.

CONFIRM
YOUR B.A.B.E. STATUS

Let's make it official. If you've read this entire book and are ready to declare yourself a B.A.B.E.—now and forever—then sign on the dotted line. Make a copy of this page and send it along with a **self-addressed stamped envelope** (with $1.50 postage) to:

> B.A.B.E.
> P.O. Box 75
> Fort Myers, FL 33902

Your B.A.B.E. ID will be mailed directly to you.

I, _____, truly believe that I'm beautiful in my heavenly Father's eyes. I'm accepted by him unconditionally. I'm blessed with spiritual gifts and special abilities that he chose for me. I'm eternally significant with a life plan that will make a difference. I'm a B.A.B.E.

I choose to develop God-Beauty. I choose to have an audience of One and to see my value based upon what God's Word says about me. I choose to develop and use my gifts and talents for God's purposes. I choose to seek God's plan for my life so I'll be eternally significant and will bring him glory.

I choose to become the kind of young woman God can use. I choose to *be* the B.A.B.E. I am.

Signature:_____

Date: _____

Email: _____

CATCH
THE B.A.B.E. WAVE!

Teen girls all over the globe are reading this book and catching the B.A.B.E. wave! They're discovering that they're B.A.B.E.s in God's eyes, in his opinion, in his kingdom! And ultimately that's *all* that matters. Girls just like you want to honor God with their lives and live out his purposes for them.

The B.A.B.E. wave is on the move! And you can help keep it rolling.

Now that *you* understand that you're a B.A.B.E., you can help other girls discover that they too are beautiful, accepted, blessed, and eternally significant. You can skyrocket their self-esteem by chatting up the fact that they were created *on* purpose and *for* a purpose.

Wherever you live, whatever your life situation, you can start right now to shape your generation by giving them a crystal clear vision of who they are in Christ and what they're here on earth to do. Life isn't meaningless—not even sorta! Pray for opportunities to tell others—cousins, classmates, teammates, co-workers. Pray for the right words at the right time. Pray for listeners' hearts to be open. And pray for your B.A.B.E. girlfriends around the world to remember *who they are* and to be courageous, knowing that God is with them as they take this message to their peers.

Live the B.A.B.E. message. Share the B.A.B.E. message. Be the B.A.B.E. message. Keep the B.A.B.E. wave rolling.

I'll be praying for you!

EXTRA STUFF 1
Spiritual Gifts List

The Bible tells us that God chooses at least one spiritual gift to give you—not exclusively, of course, but one you'll delight in using. Paul describes most of these gifts in Romans 12:6–8; 1 Corinthians 12:7–10, 28; and Ephesians 4:11–13. Read the definitions, then place a check mark by the gift(s) you may have.

Gifts in Romans

Prophecy: hearing a special "right now" message from God and speaking it to his people

Serving: recognizing jobs that need to be done and finding a way to complete them

Teaching: communicating information (by word and deed) so others can understand and grow

Exhortation: speaking words that encourage others and stimulate their faith

Giving: cheerfully and generously sharing what you have with others

Leading: catching God's vision, setting goals, and influencing others to help reach them

Mercy: genuinely feeling what others are feeling, then being sympathetic, comforting, and kind

Gifts in 1 Corinthians

Wisdom: using Holy Spirit–given insight to give wise advice right when it's needed

Knowledge: discovering, understanding, and clarifying information to help God's people

Faith: having unquenchable trust and confidence about God's plan and purposes

Healing: laying hands on ill people, praying for them, and seeing God cure them

Miracles: serving as the human instrument that receives God's power to perform powerful acts

Distinguishing of spirits: knowing if a person's spirit is of God or of Satan

Speaking in tongues: receiving and delivering a message from God through a divine language you've never learned; also used in private prayer to God

Interpreting tongues: receiving from God the translation of a message given in tongues

Prophecy: same as above

Gifts in Ephesians

Apostle: gathering believers together in a new environment

Evangelism: sharing the Good News of Jesus and winning nonbelievers to Christ

Pastoring: providing the care and spiritual feeding of God's people

Prophet and Teacher: same as above

Gifts from Other Places in Scripture

Celibacy: remaining single and sexually abstinent for purposes of serving God (1 Corinthians 7:7)

Hospitality: welcoming into your home those who need food and/or lodging (1 Peter 4:9)

Intercession: praying on behalf of others; standing in the gap (Colossians 1:9–12)

Exorcism: casting out demons using God's supernatural power (Acts 16:16–18)

Helps: working behind the scenes to assist others in fulfilling their ministry (Romans 16:1–2)

Administration: creating a plan and organizing others to complete it (Titus 1:5)

EXTRA STUFF 2
Who You Are in Christ!

*You are God's child, adopted into his family as his very own (see John 1:12; Ephesians 1:5). *It's the best family ever. You're a full-fledged member, entitled to an inheritance.*

*You are born of God, and the evil one cannot touch you (see 1 John 5:18). *You are God's property!*

*You are a member of Christ's body (see 1 Corinthians 12:27). *You are his hands and feet, his eyes and ears, here to serve.*

*You are a partaker of his divine nature (see 2 Peter 1:3–4). *You have everything you need to live a godly life.*

*You are created in God's likeness (see Genesis 1:26–27). *You have his qualities growing in you as you are faithful to seek him.*

*You are fearfully and wonderfully made (see Psalm 139:13–14). *Remember, you are not just carelessly tossed together.*

*You are chosen by Jesus and called his friend (see John 15:15–16). *You are not a slave, not a neighbor, not an acquaintance, but a friend!*

*You are the home of the Holy Spirit, who lives in you (see John 14:16–18; 1 Corinthians 6:19). *You are more than flesh and bones; you are a hangout for the Holy Spirit.*

*You are forgiven (see 1 John 1:9). *You are forgiven even when you blow it big-time, even when you do it over and over.*

*You are holy and blameless in God's sight (see Ephesians 1:4). *Sounds unimaginable, but because of Jesus, God sees you as faultless!*

*You have been bought with a price and belong to Christ (see 1 Corinthians 6:20). *Your sins were paid for in full when Jesus died on the cross.*

*You are redeemed (see Ephesians 1:14). *You've been restored and given new and everlasting value.*

*You have the righteousness of God (see 2 Corinthians 5:21). *Jesus grants us his righteousness, and we are in right standing with God.*

*You are loved (see John 3:16; Ephesians 2:4). *Even when it feels like no one else loves you, God always does.*

*You cannot be separated from God's love (see Romans 8:35–39). *No fear of rejection here.*

*You are a brand-new creation in Christ (see 2 Corinthians 5:17). *God made you new and clean on the inside—totally different.*

*You are complete in Christ (see Colossians 2:10). *Yep. You have it all—love, peace, security, kindness, joy, power, sound mind . . . You name it, it's yours.*

*You are a saint, a citizen of heaven (see 1 Corinthians 1:2–3; Philippians 3:20). *This world isn't your real home; you are on loan from the throne!*

*You have direct access to God (see Ephesians 2:18). *You don't have to use a formula or go through another person to get to God.*

*You are God's workmanship, created for good works (see Ephesians 2:10). *You're a work of art designed to do good things for Jesus!*

*You have eternal life in heaven (see 1 John 5:13). *What better place to spend forever?*

*You can do all things through Christ who strengthens you (see Philippians 4:13). *What God assigns you to do, he will help you through.*

*You are free from condemnation (see Romans 8:1–2). *Don't let anyone put you down. God has lifted you up!*

*You are protected by the power of God (see 2 Thessalonians 3:3; 1 Peter 1:5). *Ask and he will send his angels anytime!*

*Your adequacy is from God (see 2 Corinthians 3:5). *It's not about what you can do, but about what God can do through you!*

*You are sealed in Christ by the Holy Spirit of promise (see Ephesians 1:13). *Signed, sealed, and eventually delivered to heaven. If Jesus is your Lord, you are headed to heaven. It's a sure thing!*

*You have been given a spirit not of fear, but of power, love, and a sound mind (see 2 Timothy 1:7). *Forget dread, panic, worry, and timidity. You've got the power.*

*You are salt in this world (see Matthew 5:13). *Your very presence can make others thirsty for God.*

*You are a light in this world (see Matthew 5:14, 16; Ephesians 5:8). *Your love and good deeds for God make you shine and point others to the heavenly Father.*

*You have been called to bear fruit (see John 15:16). *What joy you have when you see God working in and through you.*

*You are seated with Christ in the heavenly realm (see Ephesians 2:6). *You've got spiritual royalty to the max.*

*You have been created with a plan and purpose in mind (see Psalm 139:16; Jeremiah 29:11–13). *God has your life mapped out.*

*You are victorious through Christ (see Romans 8:37). *Victory in Jesus—it's all about obedience.*

*You are called to be a witness for Christ and to make disciples (see Mark 16:15; Acts 1:8). *What an honor to tell others about Jesus and help them learn his ways.*

*You are filled with power from God (see Acts 1:8; Ephesians 3:20). *You are never dependent on your own abilities. God's power works in you.*

*You are crowned with glory and majesty (see Psalm 8:3–5). *You're a princess glowing with God's glory!*

THE GLAMOUR GIRLS "CHAT IT UP" GUIDE

When it comes to talking about beauty, most of you B.A.B.E.s don't need a guide to get the conversation rolling. Just grab a group of friends, read this book, and have fun blabbing about the topics it covers. You can get started by agreeing to read a chapter for each time you meet. Each girl can come up with questions she wants to ask or topics she wants to discuss. (I know you won't have trouble coming up with your own questions to discuss—that's why I'm not giving you any!)

Now agree on a time and place to meet together and chat it up! You're going to have a blast with this one!

Suggestion: Your chat sessions may bring up some questions you and your friends can't really answer—other than your best educated guess. Take these questions to a woman you know and trust who can help you out. Don't settle for unanswered questions; that won't help you learn.

If you want to go through this book with a leader, pray about the best woman for the job and then ask her. She'll be flattered. Then have her glance through the Glamour Girls "Chat It Up" Leader's Guide on the next page.

THE GLAMOUR GIRLS "CHAT IT UP" LEADER'S GUIDE

I've personally witnessed the phenomenon that takes place when a group of girls gets together to talk (one of their favorite pastimes). Eventually their walls come down and their hearts open up. How special to be a part of that. And what B.A.B.E. doesn't like to talk about beauty? It's great that you've chosen to be part of this by being a leader!

Now you might be wondering what exactly your role as group leader is. Here are some tips to get you started:

Andrea's Top Ten Guidelines for Leading a Chat Session

Here are some tips for enhancing your time with your group:

1. **Pray!** Pray for God's guidance as you prepare and share. Pray for each girl in your group. Pray that the eyes of her heart would be enlightened so she would know the hope of her calling (Ephesians 1:18). Pray that she would be filled with the knowledge of God's will in all spiritual wisdom and understanding so that she may walk in a manner worthy of the Lord, pleasing him in all areas of her life and bearing fruit in every good work she attempts for the Lord (Colossians 1:9–10). For those who don't know the Lord, pray that they would see their need for him and say yes to his saving grace.

2. **Be prepared!** Read through the entire book; then go back and prepare each week by reviewing the section and coming

up with some questions and topics for discussion straight out of the text. For instance:

> Why is it dangerous to experiment with vomiting, laxatives, diuretics, compulsive exercise, and drastic dieting?
>
> What are some things you can do to keep your skin fresh and clean?
>
> What are some ways you build a healthier body?
>
> What does it mean to have "real beauty"?

Be willing to share one personal story that relates to the topic of the week, yet be sensitive to the amount of time you talk about you! One or two stories can help your group open up, but too many stories may make them feel you don't want to hear about them! Balance is always the key.

3. **Welcome them!** This works best when you're the first one to arrive at the meeting spot (church, Starbucks, a restaurant). Get some tunes going, mix up some lemonade, and be ready so that when they walk through the door, your attention is on them.

4. **Encourage participation!** The first few weeks, allow your group to participate at their own comfort level. Everyone need not answer every question. Eventually it will be good if each girl shares. After all, this book is all about beauty and things girls deal with and things they have opinions on! For those shy B.A.B.E.s, rather than just calling on them and putting them on the spot, go for a gentler approach (instead of "Melissa, your turn," try "We'd love to hear how you answered that question, Melissa. Would you be willing to share?"). Now, for the girl who always has something to say and is the first one to say it, bring along some duct tape. Just kidding! Try something like, "Sarah, we like hearing your answers, but let's have someone else go first this time." Hopefully, that will help! **Important:** Every answer matters! No response

is too insignificant. Do your best to validate and affirm their answers.

5. **Be genuine!** Ask questions with interest and warmth. Maintain as much eye contact with the group as possible (especially with the girl who's talking). Be conscious of your facial expressions and body language (smiling is good; nodding off is bad).

6. **Go deeper!** If you want them to elaborate on an answer or you don't quite understand what they're saying, try phrases like, "Tell us more about that." "Why do you feel that way?" "How did that make you feel?" "What did you learn from that situation?" "What would you do differently next time?" "When you say _____, what does that mean to you?"

7. **Be creative!** Add visual aids like magazine ads, movie clips, props, posters, book excerpts, skits, role playing, and more! Use your imagination. It keeps the learning fun for you and them!

8. **Let the Spirit lead!** Commit each week to the Lord. If the lesson seems to be going in a different direction or if your group seems intent on one aspect of the lesson, be willing to forgo the plan, trusting that the Spirit wants to work in the girls' lives right then. It's important to discern between the Holy Spirit's direction, a rabbit trail, and one girl getting on her soap box! But if there's sincere interaction, go with it. There might even be someone who becomes visibly upset or tearful. Feel free to stop to pray for her. Follow up by asking her if there's anything she needs or if there's anything you can do to help.

9. **Welcome silence!** I realize that five seconds can feel like five hours when you toss out a question and suddenly no one has a thing to say! Don't panic—allow them time to process the question and think about their answers. If necessary, reword the question and toss it out again.

10. **Be brave!** Two thoughts here. First, in a group of teen girls, there will be differences in opinion, levels of experi-

ence, and spiritual maturity. Allow for it and expect it. Do your best to highlight answers that are closest to the biblical point of view. Second, there are bound to be questions you can't answer. There may even be someone in the group who actually gets a kick out of trying to stump you! Believe me, I've been there. I encourage you to turn it into a positive and congratulate them for really thinking hard! It shows they're hungry for truth. Write down the question, and do your best to have an answer the next week. You might even challenge the group to search their Bibles ("What does the Bible say about beauty?") or poll girls at school ("What percentage of girls are 100 percent happy with the way they look?") so that you can dig for the answer together.

Playing by the Rules!

Here are some simple rules to share with your small group:

Keep it confidential. What's shared in the group stays in the group.

Avoid judging. Respect the views of others.

Don't fix it. Offer advice only if it's requested.

No interrupting. Whoever's speaking, let her finish.

Take turns. Don't do all the talking. We learn more by listening.

Pray for group members. It's the kindest and most powerful thing you can do.

Getting Started!

Secure a copy of *Glamour Girls* for each participant. Have Bibles, pens/pencils, and extra paper handy. Have a sign-in sheet—include name, address, phone number, and email address. Challenge yourself to memorize the girls' names ASAP. Personally contacting them a few times during the course of the study means the world to them. Send a note or an email or give them a call. If you have more than ten girls, recruit another leader and have two groups. You know your group best. Focus in on their needs.

Try This Lineup!

Hey, Glad You're Here! (greet them)

Get Those Pretty Little Heads Thinking! (general opening question)

Invite Jesus to Join You! (opening prayer)

What's God Up To? (praise reports/testimonies)

Hide It in Your Heart! (memory verse)

And the Answer Is . . . ! (Q & A)

Change and Rearrange! (personal application)

Wrap It Up! (closing prayer)

What's Up Next Week! (assignment and memory verse)

Know who you are!

You were created *on* purpose *for* a purpose!

Here's your chance to become a **b**eautiful, **a**ccepted, **b**lessed, and **e**ternally significant **B.a.B.e.**!

Get the **inside dish** from these **divine divas!**

Learn to live out your faith every day by
following the examples of these godly women.

Baffled by boys?

andrea stephens

BOYLAND

A B.a.B.e.'S° GUIDE TO UNDERSTANDING GUYS

Get awesome advice, solid information, and powerful tools
that will rock your relationship with guys!